About this book

The Cambridge Amateur Swimming Club, Jesus Green Baths, circa 1932

THIS BOOK WAS inspired by the centenary of Jesus Green Lido. It celebrates 100 years of swimming at our unique pool, through the voices of its swimmers. The book contains a newly researched history of the Lido, interviews with winter and summer swimmers, paintings, photographs and poems as well as invited contributions. They create a vivid picture of the special place Jesus Green Lido holds in our hearts, and of its warm welcome for future swimmers.

ANNIE MORGAN JAMES & BECKY ALLEN

100 YARDS, 100 VOICES

A CENTURY OF SWIMMING AT JESUS GREEN LIDO

EDITED BY BECKY ALLEN, SARA LEDWITH & COLIN CAMPBELL

First published 2024
by The Lane Publishing
www.thelanepublishing.com

1

ISBN: 9781068769801

Text copyright © Annie Morgan James and Becky Allen 2024

The right of Annie Morgan James and Becky Allen to be identified as the authors of this work has been asserted by them in accordance with the Copyright, Designs and Patents Act 1988.

All rights reserved.
No part of this publication may be reproduced, stored in a retrieval system, or transmitted in any form, or by any means, electronic, mechanical, photocopying, recording or otherwise, without permission in writing from the publisher.

A CIP catalogue record for this book is available from the British Library.

Designed and published by The Lane Publishing, Cambridge.

Printed and bound by Langham Press, Cambridge.

Published with support from Cambridge City Council, Better, Anglia Ruskin University and the Friends of Jesus Green Lido.

Many of the images used in this book were supplied by the contributors, and the authors gratefully acknowledge these individuals' additional contribution and permission to use these images. For a list of additional picture credits see page 202.

Cover: Filling the pool for the 2021 season, Martin Bond
Inside front cover, left to right: Elizabeth Pickett, Eleanor Thomas, Alice Hibbert
Inside back cover, left to right: On Ki Angel Chak, Michael Tyrrell, Eve Jacques
Back cover: 1 January 2020, Martin Bond

For Mark Goodson

About the authors

DR ANNIE MORGAN James has lived in Cambridge with her family for over 30 years. A swimmer all her life, she was delighted to discover when she first arrived in the city that Jesus Green Lido was her local pool. Since then, she has been a regular swimmer throughout the year, and she is now a committee member of the Friends of Jesus Green Lido. She is a lecturer in the Faculty of Arts, Humanities, Education and Social Sciences, at Anglia Ruskin University. Her research interests are film, history and identity. She loves swimming and flamenco.

BECKY ALLEN IS a swimmer and journalist covering science, the environment and cycling. She has had a lifelong love of swimming. As a baby, her first swims were in the Solent at Southsea. As an adult, her favourite swims include the Feldberger Seenlandschaft, north of Berlin, and Hathersage Pool in the Peak District. In 1990 she came to Cambridge planning to stay for 18 months. After meeting her partner, Mark Goodson, and discovering Jesus Green Lido it became impossible to leave. Her passion for swimming, the Lido and its community has made writing this book with Annie Morgan James a pleasure and a privilege.

Foreword

IT'S NO ACCIDENT that so many contributors to this centenary celebration of Jesus Green Lido talk about it in the language of devotion. They call it paradise, a godsend, a haven, a sanctuary, a life saver. And they are not wrong, for Jesus Green is much more than a swimming pool. It is a wellspring of health and happiness. Glittering between the river and the trees, it is an oasis of tranquillity (no canned music!) at the centre of a bursting city. It is a source of mental as well as physical fitness. And this long stretch of blue water harbours a community – friendly, unpretentious, diverse and democratic – which embodies the utopian spirit of the place.

As appears in the brief history of the Jesus Green pool that follows, its survival was far from certain. Built when the benefits of fresh air, sunshine and exercise were being proclaimed after the First World War, it anticipated the boom in lido construction during the 1930s. The bust came during the 1980s, largely owing to government restrictions on local authority spending, and since then matters have not improved. By 2005 Greater London alone had lost 42 of its 50 outdoor swimming pools, and since 2010 more than 400 pools have closed in England as a whole. Jesus Green Lido itself was threatened with extinction and there was even talk of putting a car park in its place. Yet thanks mainly to the dedication and determination of the Friends of Jesus Green Lido, it was saved.

Today it flourishes as never before, a fact illustrated in the following pages which form a rich tapestry of testimony. The Covid crisis demonstrated its worth in terms of well-being. Winter opening has proved, at least to hardy souls, the value of cold swimming.

Better lives up to its name and ensures safe bathing, especially for children. When they are not splashing about or powering the lanes, adults enjoy the idyllic surroundings.

Having swum in the Lido for well over half its 100-year existence, I hope this volume will help to ensure that it lives on for centuries to come. Future generations should experience the bliss of being cradled in the arms of Jesus Green Lido.

PIERS BRENDON

Introduction

LIDOS ARE PRECIOUS facilities which in recent years have grown in popularity and are being restored and preserved for communities of swimmers throughout the country.

I remember the first time I saw Jesus Green Lido – a blue oasis by the banks of the River Cam. Swimming had defined my childhood and, growing up in Edinburgh, I spent summers swimming at Portobello Lido and winters in my local baths, but I had never seen such a magical, long pool of inviting water. Moving to Cambridge as an adult and discovering Jesus Green Lido immediately brought back those happy days of watery freedom.

I have swum here for over 30 years with my mum, my husband, my daughter and stepdaughters, grandchildren, friends and alone – so many swimming memories and so many swims to look forward to in the years ahead.

This book is a tribute to Jesus Green Lido through the voices of its swimmers past and present. In researching the history and gathering the memories, pictures and paintings, I found the strong tie which unites us all is the community the pool has created. This is a place that is cherished – a precious aquatic facility like no other – the people's pool.

Annie Morgan James

WHEN WE EMBARKED on this book to celebrate Jesus Green Lido's centenary, we had only a vague notion of the shape it might take. We wanted to research a definitive history of the pool, to speak to 100 swimmers about this 100-yard pool as it turned 100, and we trusted these words would flow together into something special.

And so they have. This book contains reflections from more than 100 swimmers; intimate stories, told with openness and honesty. They are individual stories about a singular pool. They are also universal stories of outdoor swimming communities everywhere. They hold the joys of childhood, family, sunny summers and rites of passage, but also loss, struggle and sadness.

During the 35 years I have lived in Cambridge, the Lido has been my safe space, swimmers my tribe. The day after we finished the first draft of this book, my partner died while I was swimming. Since then, swimmers at the Lido have met me with quiet care and compassion. The Lido has given me breathing space. The water holds me up.

The Lido gives us all these things. Thank you Jesus Green Lido.

Becky Allen

Contents

A History   1

The People's Pool   11
Arthur Mansfield, Christine Jarvis, Michael Heffer and Lucy Hines, Peter Gilmour and the Pink Floyd Connection, Lionel Langford, Colin Beckett, Ruth Eckstein, Tim Verney

Reflections   27
Anne Garvey, Bronwen Dinneen, Joan Ludman, David Firman, Jassy Marshall, Mary Williams, Philip Boulding KC, Tom Woodcock, Saul Betmead de Chasteigner, Lynn Morgan, Rosie Tween, Ruth Barnett, Steve Tunnicliffe-Wilson, Sue Rogers, Conrad Lichtenstein

Into the Cold   49
Anna-Rose Harris, Hamra Yucel, Danya Harris, David Rees, Elaine Brown, Di Beddow, Ellie Standen, Pilvi Saarikoski, Simone Schnall, Emily Spence

Generations   65
Alice Smith, Arlo Burton, Max Wildman, Grace and Alice Wilson, Ellen Wilson, Gabriel McGovern, Sophie Grove, Ysmay Gill, Duncan Black, Grace and Tom Twinley, Julie Ling, Naomi Worth, Robin and Fiona Todd, Ellen Nowak and Family, Carole Ellison, Ruby Reed, Natty Barnett

Community   79
Duncan Gibson, Emma Bateman, Melissa Santiago-Val, Suzanna Watson, Penny Wilson, Sinéad Ryan, Sue Gordon-Roe, Catherine Hayhurst, Laura Turvill, Jane Firman, In Memoriam: Nina Hallowell by Ginny Morrow, Maurizio Cavaliere

Friendship   93
Charlie Roberts, Jane Woodin, Jane Keate, Martin Lown, Katy McLarnon, Ruth Barnett, Vicky Bursa, Francis Jeans, Lisa Turvill, Carlos Toranzos, Paul Morgan, Meg Platt, Eleanor Godfrey

Challenge   115
Dirk Gewert, Evie Anema, Sophie Etheridge, Kate Downes, Sarah Cox, David Lynch, Lindsay James, Greg Alvey, Jo-Anne Fowles, Simon Timberlake, Sylvia Ferdin, Lawrence Dixon, Esther Chambers, Suzanne Desmond, Sara Ledwith, Sam Thorogood, Rebecca Taylor, Sarah Blower

Guardian Angels   139
Finn Barnes, Gabriele Scarmatto, Kane Smith, George Pemberton, Daryl Emes, Julie Durrant, Ian Ross, Colin Campbell, Mary Cotton, Alex Buxton, Nicky Blanning, Val Moore

Celebrations   169
A Year of Celebration, Orla Moore, Centenary Cygnets, Chris Hudson, Rosina Piovani, The Flag Project, Har Hari Kaur, Eleanor Thomas, Michael Tyrrell, Zoe Mogridge, Frances Ives, Tanya Jones, Leigh Chambers, Tom Ling

Acknowledgements   190

References   191

A HISTORY

The swimmers bike to Jesus Green on bicycles with fins and tails, some drive in cars that look like whales through traffic lights of ocean green[1]

CAMBRIDGE'S HISTORY IS intertwined with swimming. The River Cam, which winds its way through the city, has long facilitated a culture of bathing. It was Everard Digby, a Latin scholar and fellow of St John's College, who in 1587 wrote one of the first published guides to swimming.

Titled *The Art of Swimming*, Digby's book wanted to "provide his readers with the means to learn how to propel, manoeuvre and enjoy themselves in the water."[2] Originally written in Latin and translated into English in 1595, it was the first book entirely devoted to reconnecting the Renaissance world with water, giving readers the tools, knowledge and practical advice to get into the swim.[3]

Cambridge is home to Britain's two oldest purpose-built outdoor pools, whose origins lie in the 17th century. The pools are situated in secluded corners of the grounds at Christ's College and Emmanuel College.[4] The University's associations with river swimming run deep. Lord Byron, Rupert Brooke, and Virginia Woolf[5] were all regular river bathers, and the Cam remains popular with river swimmers today.

The English passion for swimming has long marked them out, according to Charles Sprawson in his classic 1992 memoir *Haunts of the Black Masseur: the Swimmer as Hero*. "In the nineteenth century the English were acknowledged as the best swimmers in the world," he says, "at a time when passion for athleticism and for games became their distinguishing feature and made them the object of fascination to the rest of Europe."[6]

The Channel Swimming Association was founded in 1927, more than 50 years after Captain Webb became the first man to swim the English Channel in 1875. Swimming clubs had sprung up throughout the mid- to late 1800s, and the Amateur Swimming Association was established in 1886 with Queen Victoria as patron. It was not until the 1920s, however, that a journal dedicated solely to aquatic sports – *The Swimming Times* – emerged. Swimming had, clearly, come into its own.[7]

Swimming had been a competitive sport since the first Olympic Games of the modern era in 1896. For the London 1908 Olympics, a 100-metre outdoor pool was built in the centre of the Olympic Stadium in Shepherd's Bush. The British men took gold in water polo, four of the six swimming gold medals on offer, two silvers and a bronze.[8] Such a legacy surely meant swimming for all.

In Cambridge, swimming was as important for the town as for the

Jesus Green Bath.

Chronicle Photos.]
Our top picture gives a capital view of the new public bath on Jesus Green, opened by the Mayor (Councillor G. H. Lavender) on Thursday. Its length is 300 feet, and its breadth 40 feet. The bottom picture shows the finish of the first race over the full course, and a view of the large crowd. Inset is the Mayor making his speech by the aid of a megaphone.

The formal opening of Jesus Green Baths, 30 August 1923

University. People swam in the length of the River Cam between Sheep's Green and Coe Fen in Newnham. Men and women bathed at different locations. Men and boys used the river at Sheep's Green, while women swam in a more protected place from bathing sheds built by the local council in 1896.

Generations of children learned to swim in the Cam, many of them taught by Charles Driver in a sidestream known as the Snobs.[9] The city's swimming club, the Cambridge Amateur Swimming Club, founded in 1906, organised summer swimming competitions[10] in the city and surrounding villages such as Prickwillow.

By 1918, swimming pools had become ubiquitous across urban England, competitive swimming was highly organised and swimming had become widely accepted "as a pleasurable activity which was both good for the individual and for society as a whole."[11]

Physical cleanliness was associated with moral cleanliness, and municipal pools played an important role in democratising and popularising swimming for the masses. According to Agnes Campbell's report for the Carnegie United Kingdom Trust on the state of public baths in 1918, "Among the forms of recreation which are possible under cramped conditions, swimming necessarily occupies a very high place. It is recognised as a first-rate physical exercise, owing to the muscular training it affords, and the tonic effect of contact with cold water. It calls for a certain amount of pluck and endurance."[12]

As the wave of open-air pools began to be built across the UK in the early 20th century, it was natural that Cambridge should have one on the banks of the River Cam. Punting had also become a pleasure activity on the Cam and a pool was a way of diverting the swimmers from the river. Moreover, seeking ways to provide work during a period of high unemployment – as well as providing the population with a pool – Cambridge City Council set aside £3,000 at a special meeting in September 1921 for the construction of a bathing pool.[13]

The Cambridge Corporation Act 1922 gave the Council greater control over common land, enabling them to build a pool on a chosen location. There followed heated debate about where along the river the pool should be built, with two potential sites – Jesus Green and Morley's Holt further downstream – emerging as front runners.

Those in favour of Jesus Green argued that water from the stream at Morley's Holt was not always as good for bathing, and that Jesus Green was more accessible for a large number of schools.[14] Opponents said a pool would spoil the beauty of Jesus Green Common. At a Council meeting in January 1923, Councillor Stevens, one of the main supporters of the Jesus Green

> **" Jesus Green Bath would eventually break with convention by offering mixed bathing, albeit only on Sunday mornings**

The Cambridge Amateur Swimming Club, Jesus Green Baths, circa 1930

site, sought to allay fears a pool would be an eyesore.

The meeting provided light relief for the *Cambridge Chronicle and University Journal*, which reported on Stevens' speech. "He considered the ladies' bathing place there a pretty view. (Laughter) 'I know what you are laughing at. You are laughing about seeing the ladies bobbing up and down' – (renewed laughter) – 'but I am not, I am considering the site. Never mind, I am glad it's pleasing some of you. I still maintain that it is a prettier sight – not counting the ladies – than when it was a poor old Common, and nothing planted there.'"[15]

Although women and men had separate bathing places on the river, Councillor Few, another advocate for the Jesus Green site, daringly argued in 1923 for mixed bathing: "They should remove the barrier between the sexes [as] there was sufficient barrier already," he was cited in the *Chronicle* as saying.[16] Jesus Green Bath would eventually break with convention by offering mixed bathing, albeit only on Sunday mornings (7am–10am) and weekday afternoons (4.30pm–6pm). Women and men had separate entrances. Proposals for two pools – one for women and another for men – were dropped, but help explain why both ends of the pool are shallow but the middle is deep.

With the site decided, the pool was dug by local men returning from World War One who, according to one of the pool's first swimmers – Arthur Mansfield – went on strike for a farthing but lost their jobs instead.[17]

At 100 yards long, the pool along with Tooting Bec Lido in London became the longest in the country. Its width, however, was just 15 yards, so its long and slender shape would mimic swimming in the River Cam nearby, according to a news report. The pool was filled with water from the river. Small fish would be spotted by swimmers.[18] Dogs were also

The Cambridge Amateur Swimming Club, Jesus Green Baths, 1928

allowed to swim in Jesus Green Bath as they did in the river.

On 30 August 1923, Jesus Green Bath was formally opened by the Mayor (Councillor G.H. Lavender) of Cambridge who declined to swim. Under the headline 'Big Splash at the Bath,' the *Chronicle* reported that "although he and the mayoress liked water, they liked it warm."[19] Among the public, however, there was huge enthusiasm, with people from all corners of Cambridge attracted to the opening.

"Quite fifteen hundred people lined the backs of the new baths at Chesterton on Thursday to witness the formal opening by the Mayor and a short programme of aquatic sports, arranged by the Cambridge Amateur Swimming Club, followed by an instructive life-saving demonstration," the *Chronicle* reported.[20]

Jesus Green Bath opened in an era of enormous change. The First World War and the Spanish flu epidemic had wiped out a generation of young men and left few families unscathed. Unemployment hit an all-time high of more than 1 million[21], creating areas of grinding poverty. Those who endured needed a healthier, more optimistic future. The 1920s was also a period of social and cultural development, the age of modernism and a time of technological change, the most important being the wireless, with the first BBC broadcast in 1922. In literature, established forms were being challenged, and change permeated social and cultural values. In this atmosphere, attitudes were changing towards sport, recreation and wellbeing. As a result, writes journalist and swimmer Janet Smith in *Liquid Assets*, "the open-air pool of the 20th century was a product of ideology as much as it was a fashion

> **"FANCY SWIMMING"**
>
> On 13 July 1927, the Cambridge Amateur Swimming Club, whose scrapbooks of the late 1920s and early 1930s survive in the Cambridgeshire Collection at the Central Library, organised an annual swimming sports evening at the Corporation Bathing Pool (Jesus Green). It featured 14 events including:
> - the inter-schools relay (under 14),
> - scratch races for under 16s,
> - 100 yards schools championship (14 and under) won by Milton Road,
> - an open diving competition (ladies) scooped by Ms LN Hyde with 52.5 points,
> - 500 yards championship of Cambridgeshire for the Rouse Ball Challenge Cup won by Mr RF Grundy in 8 mins 19 secs,
> - 100 yards ladies championship,
> - 50 yards club race (fully clothed),
> - an exhibition of diving, fancy swimming and lifesaving,
> - 50 yards club race (ladies),
> - 50 yards championship of Cambridgeshire won by ABG Stephen in 29 secs,
> - 100 yards club handicap (men)
> - and a water polo match between Cambridge Amateur Swimming Club and Newmarket Swimming Club.

or paternalistic concern for the welfare of the poor."[22]

Built a decade before Britain's heyday of lido building in the 1930s, the Jesus Green Bath was innovative. A leading example of how swimming brings together people from all walks of life, it was a great leveller, providing a democratic community for swimmers of all ages, abilities and backgrounds.

THE CREATION OF Jesus Green Bath was part of this new awareness. Ideas also flowed in from Europe – from Germany in particular – about the regenerative powers of such athleticism. At the formal opening of Jesus Green Bath's first full summer season on 1 May 1924, the Mayor highlighted the health benefits the new facility offered.

Reported the *Cambridge Daily News*:

"The Mayor, on declaring the Bath open to the public, expressed his pleasure and approval of the progress that had been made there recently. He went on to say that they had at the Bath two thoroughly capable and efficient instructors and it was, he thought, an excellent thing and quite safe for parents … to enjoy and receive instruction in such a healthy recreation and sport."[23]

The Bath also brought town and gown together. Cambridge already had the people's river; now it had the people's pool.

During its first decades, the pool was used for swimming lessons, galas, water polo matches and, in the 1930s, a full-time custodian opened the pool for a traditional Christmas Day party. Children attending primary schools in the local area learned to swim at Jesus Green[24] and have continued to do so through the decades.

One of Cambridge's most famous swimmers, Jack Overhill, was a great example of somebody who combined swimming in both the river and Jesus Green Bath. He was a working-class autodidact, writer and diarist who helped found the Granta Swimming Club in 1932 "to teach unemployed and impoverished men" to swim. He established an annual swim from the Mill Pond to Grantchester Meadow. He taught himself "the crawl" after seeing Jack Lavender, a Cambridge man who had learned the new style in London, swim the revolutionary stroke in the river.[25]

Overhill entered many competitions and galas, his own wins including the inaugural 50 yards race at the formal opening. His close friend Bill Clee became the Bath's first custodian.[26] A passionate swimmer, Overhill reminded himself in his diaries: "Don't forget that first and last in life – and it takes precedence over everything – writing, reading, sex and the rest of it – I'm a swimmer right to the marrow in my bones."[27]

His children too became enthusiastic swimmers. Jack Overhill junior was filmed in a display of diving at the Jesus Green Bath, 'The Four-Year-Older'[28] for Pathé News in 1932. Cinema adverts described him as "the swimming prodigy" and the "four-year-old merman,"[29] in a newsreel screened "far and wide".[30] Jack senior received many letters of congratulation on his son's performance, and the beautiful black and white newsreel captured the pool's special ambience, which remains unchanged today.

Through the decades that followed, Jesus Green Bath opened every summer from May to September. In the early years the Cambridge Amateur Swimming Association and the custodian, who looked after the premises, organised annual Christmas day swims, water polo tournaments, galas, and events at the pool became an important part of the Cambridge social calendar.

In 1956 the pool was converted from being fed with river water to a closed-pump system fed with mains water. Today, the pool takes five days to fill and holds 2,400,000 litres of water.

Many Cambridge school children

> **To swim is to be reborn. Each dive into the water is a leap of faith. Each stroke draws you closer to some nebulous goal**

learned to swim here. Local schools such as St Luke's Primary, Milton Road Primary and the Manor Secondary timetabled swimming at Jesus Green Pool during the summer term, and many baby boomers remember shivering in the shallow ends. Dating and hanging out with friends at Jesus Green throughout the summer became a rite of passage for many teenagers growing up in Cambridge.

Indoor swimming arrived in Cambridge in 1963 when Parkside pool opened, and lured by warmer water, swimming lessons and galas left Jesus Green. But the pool continued to be popular through the

1960s and 70s during the warm summer months, and in the famously hot summer of 1976, people flooded to it. *Cambridge Evening News* reported, "since the heatwave began more than 4,000 customers each weekend have passed through the turnstile."[31]

But later, like lidos up and down the country, Jesus Green suffered a drastic drop in numbers when people preferred to holiday abroad or simply found the water too cold. In 1987, following difficulties in recruiting staff, soldiers were drafted in from the Royal Engineers at Waterbeach Barracks. Speaking to *Cambridge Evening News*, Major Mike Mosedale of the Royal Engineers said: "The soldiers work on a shift system at Waterbeach swimming pool, and decided they could help the management down at Jesus Green in their spare time."[32]

In the 1990s, in response to Council discussions about cutting costs by shortening the summer opening, a group of Jesus Green Pool devotees established the Friends of Jesus Green Swimming Pool (Lido) to protect the pool and to give regular swimmers a voice. In 1997, the facilities were upgraded with new showers and loos. The following year, Jesus Green celebrated its 75th anniversary.

It kept opening every summer into the 21st century, when many of its contemporaries had long since closed their doors.

Friends of Jesus Green Pool grew in numbers as the city itself was expanding. In 2005 Chris Cox, a regular swimmer, made a beautiful short film of the Lido through its summer season, capturing its unique ambience and the turn of the year through pool draining, cleaning, preparation and filling in the spring, to the falling leaves in the autumn. Focusing on characters and movement, Chris was interested in the inspiration the pool provided: "People of all ages, shapes and sizes come to the pool to swim and socialise – and the artists also come, to paint, make music, write poetry."[33]

The film was shown at the Arts Picturehouse as part of the 25th Cambridge Film Festival in July 2005, and in 2010 the Lido itself became a venue for the Cambridge Film Festival. That September, at the end of the swimming season, the Lido was turned into an aquatic cinema. With screens at either end and some of the audience floating in punts from the River Cam, "the pool itself [was] filled with light,"[34] according to the *News*.

In *Waterlog: a swimmer's journey through Britain*, Roger Deakin wrote: "In Cambridge, beside the Cam at Jesus Green, the Lido seems to run to infinity, bordered by a row of tall limes you can gaze into as you swim."[35]

For more than 100 years, it has brought joy and solace, community and belonging to generations of swimmers of all shapes and sizes.

Today – as in 1923 – Jesus Green Lido continues to welcome and unite us as a community of swimmers. Or, as journalist and architectural historian Christopher Beanland observes in *Lido: a dip into outdoor swimming pools*: "To swim is to be reborn. Each dive into the water is a leap of faith. Each stroke draws you closer to some nebulous goal. Each breath reinforces your sense of sentient humanity."[36]

Annie Morgan James

THE PEOPLE'S POOL

ARTHUR MANSFIELD

IN 100 YEARS, Jesus Green Lido has brought together a bright patchwork of swimming enthusiasts, including locals, children, scholars, dons, music celebrities, popstars, Olympians, Channel swimmers, triathletes, visitors and Arthur Mansfield.

On the official opening day hundreds of children thronged the pool. Arthur, at 13, was one. Arthur would not only swim on the first day but throughout his long life, remaining a regular into his 90s. For Jesus Green Pool's 75th anniversary in 1998, Arthur vividly recalled the 1923 opening.

"I was living off Mill Road. Word got around that the pool had opened. We rushed over and had a swim. It was tremendously exciting. I had already learnt to swim in the Cam at Sheep's Green."

You can feel the excitement in Arthur's description and his connection with both the River Cam and the Lido. Arthur had been taught to swim by the legendary Charlie Driver, custodian of the town bathing sheds.

Arthur's words highlight the Bath's importance in helping children to learn to swim, away from the mud and weeds of the river.

He and his friends were delighted to take the plunge but, as he recalled, many children could not afford to pay to swim: "There were as many swimmers in the river as in the pool. Lots of children didn't have the entrance charge, although it was only a penny."

Many children would later enjoy free sessions on a Saturday afternoon. Throughout the pool's history, children

would learn to swim at Jesus Green. As an adult, Arthur moved to Kimberley Road, Chesterton, five minutes' walk from Jesus Green Lido, and continued swimming every season throughout his life.

Speaking to the *Cambridge Evening News* in 1987, he said: "I feel like Rothschild in here," as he surveyed the Lido. He loved the water, the ambience and the people.

Arthur is fondly remembered by fellow regular and neighbour Michael Heffer and his daughter Lucy Hines (page 14).

> ❝ Word got around that the pool had opened. We rushed over and had a swim. It was tremendously exciting

Bathers and their dogs, Jesus Green Baths, circa 1930

CHRISTINE JARVIS

CHRISTINE WAS A young swimmer from the Arbury in Cambridge who, as a schoolgirl at the Manor Secondary Modern, swam at Jesus Green Pool in the 1960s.

The sixth fastest woman in the world over 100 metres breaststroke in 1972, she won bronze at the 1970 Commonwealth Games in Edinburgh and competed in the 1974 Commonwealth Games and at the Olympics in 1972 and 1976.

Just before the Montreal Olympics in 1976 a fan of Christine's wrote to the *Cambridge Evening News* extolling her achievements: "It was tremendous news to read that Christine Jarvis had broken the British 100 metres breaststroke record and the fact that now in her mid-twenties, a time when most top swimmers have retired, she is to represent her country at the Olympic Games. One can only conjure up a picture of sheer determination."

Christine trained in Bedford and with the elite British swimming squad in the early 1970s, but she was an exceptional role model for many young Cambridge swimmers.

MICHAEL HEFFER & LUCY HINES

Michael Heffer was born in Suffolk and moved to Cambridge in 1963, where he lived with his family until his death in 2023. He worked as an architect for Cambridgeshire County Council, taking early retirement at the age of 50, when he retrained as a violin maker at Welsh School of Musical Instrument Making at Abertridwr. Talented, curious and steadfast, Michael loved cycling, working on his allotment, and Jesus Green Lido, where he swam for almost 60 years. Speaking at his grandfather's funeral, Frankie Hines said, "He kept going to the swimming pool until he couldn't get up the steps anymore, and took a dip in the sea at Aldeburgh well after the point when we'd started to wonder if it was wise to."

Michael Heffer, wife Veronica and daughters Charlotte and Lucy, Jesus Green Pool, 1963

MICHAEL

THREE GENERATIONS OF our family have swum at Jesus Green Pool, but no great-grandchildren yet! I was swimming right up until lockdown and if it hadn't been for that, I would have gone on my mobility scooter. Jesus Green Pool was a regular social meeting place, and it was very democratic. It was one of the most important places in my life.

In 1962, we were moving to Cambridge from Chichester and I was looking for a place for us to live, walking by the river past the Fort St George, and discovered the pool. It was one of the best discoveries – an opportunity to swim in an open-air pool – and it became a favourite in the summer. I taught the children to swim.

Arthur Mansfield, who was a boy in 1923, told me the pool was excavated by hand and the spoil was taken away by horse and cart, and the workers there who did the excavation went on strike for an extra farthing (equivalent to 0.05p in today's money).

I just remembered that I heard from someone who used to work as an architect for the city council that after the Second World War, the Jesus Green Pool changing rooms were built with wood donated by the Canadian government.

I used to swim at lunchtime because I worked as an architect in Shire Hall. More often than not I would meet my wife Veronica there with our daughters Lucy and Charlotte. I'd come down with my workmates and have a swim and we'd go back to work, leaving my family to enjoy an afternoon at the pool. It is a very social centre and we got to know quite a few of the regulars.

Michael Heffer's watercolours of Jesus Green Pool

There were some great characters. People like Vangie Thorgerson, the mother of Storm Thorgerson (the graphic designer who worked closely with Pink Floyd). Vangie was statuesque and had a long blonde plait – we called her Brunhilda; Valerie Pearl, the historian and second President of New Hall College; and David-six-lengths who was an accountant and lived in Humberstone Road. He was a bachelor and prided himself on swimming this distance every day.

There was also Dr Eckstein who was amazing, and she swam until she was over 100 years old. She was very brave. There was also Leila the dancer and Margo who was married to a well known writer. Then of course there was Arthur Mansfield. He was always the man down the other end, because he never ventured into the women's end. We became great friends.

Then Mary Williams came and she was so friendly, chatting to everyone. When custodian Lionel Langford was there it was managed by two people – Mrs Rose on the desk and Lionel. He did all the attendance to the water, banishing the troublesome swimmers for example, if there were boisterous boys misbehaving Lionel would dive in the pool and get them out himself. Lionel apparently, according to my wife Veronica, used to let her and her friend swim in winter and sometimes they broke the ice. After Lionel went, the pool really deteriorated.

During the 70s there were lots of moves by people to close it – there were various suggestions to concrete half of it – and as a result there were petitions trying to keep it open. It was taken over and more or less run by students. The man in charge was a local law student at Downing College

Lucy and her drawing of the diving boards at Jesus Green Pool from her childhood scrapbook, circa 1964

called Phil Baldy. He once dived off the roof of the office into the pool.

The management by students didn't last long and the army from Waterbeach briefly took over (for one season) before Empire Leisure took over. Empire also managed Coldham's Common pool (on the site of what is now the Abbey Pool). I remember that they had an engineer who used to let his dog swim in the pool. Then it was run by another company, and they introduced discount season cards for local residents.

Later, we met Alex Buxton when she was pregnant with her second daughter and used to swim with Miranda, her elder daughter. Alex started the Friends of Jesus Green Swimming Pool.

My daughter Lucy had a neighbour who used to swim up and down the pool wearing a baseball cap, sunglasses and lipstick, singing, 'Oh what a beautiful morning.'

I used to swim every day, weather permitting, and I would do both crawl and breaststroke. I could swim for about a mile, but generally I swam five lengths.

LUCY

I REMEMBER SWIMMING in a gala and winning a race – the first time I won anything in my life! After school we used to come to the pool to meet boys. One time my mum and dad had to come and collect me because I was so late coming home. I had been kissing a boy under the bridge!

The pool has been great for lots of families through the generations. Young families would bring their babies and small children. In the 1960s my mum's friend brought her baby in a basket under the seat and Alex Buxton and I brought our children.

We went all day. If I hadn't had that pool, I don't know what I would have done – it was a life saver.

I always say Jesus Green Pool isn't just about swimming, it is the social side of things, the community.

> How I wish, how I wish you were here
> We're just two lost souls swimming in a fish bowl
> Year after year

Lyrics by Roger Waters

WISH YOU WERE HERE: THE PINK FLOYD CONNECTION

The iconic musicians from 1960s psychedelic band Pink Floyd – Roger Waters, Syd Barrett and Dave Gilmour – grew up in Cambridge and as teenagers along with friends such as Storm Thorgerson (graphic designer and music filmmaker) frequented Jesus Green Lido in the summer season.

Libby Gausden, Syd Barrett's first girlfriend, recalls meeting him when they were both teenagers: "We met on Jesus Green. There was a huge open-air swimming pool there which we all had membership of and we'd all swim from April to September to get our money's worth."

PETER GILMOUR

I FIRST WENT to Jesus Green at the age of 11 and up until my 20s. I left Cambridge to live in London in 1970. Over the years, when I return to the city, if I have my swimming togs I'll go to JG for a swim. It is a special place.

At first I went with the Boy Scouts in the early 60s and then with different groups of friends in the summer. It seemed new then, so I am surprised it is 100 years old. I think the pump room was quite new… I also remember all the trees surrounding the pool.

I learned to swim at the Snobs (a shallow part of the Cam at Sheep's Green) in Newnham and swam both in the river and Jesus Green. Jesus Green was the place to go on a sunny day in the summer to swim up and down, sun yourself at the top end and enjoy the cafe.

We used to spend afternoons sitting around talking and sometimes nip through the hedge to the swings and then come back again. I remember Lionel Langford, the custodian; he had also been the custodian at the Snobs in Newnham.

He was a big authoritative man and wore a vest and wouldn't stand any nonsense.

It was a meeting place. I remember going with David, my brother, and meeting Libby (Syd Barrett's girlfriend). I went out with her sister Judy. Both sisters belonged to the Granta swimming club.

LIONEL LANGFORD

Lionel Langford was a Lido legend. As custodian of Jesus Green in the 1960s and 70s, he taught a generation of Cambridge kids to swim and ensured they were safe in the water. Stern when called for, he had a fine repertoire of one liners, according to his daughter-in-law Julie Langford, and Colin Beckett, of University Cycles on Victoria Road, Cambridge.

Lido legend Lionel Langford

L IONEL ALWAYS LOVED having a laugh and a joke. He never minded people enjoying themselves but anything anywhere near dangerous would get you the sharp end of his tongue. He had been known to ban people for a while if they went too far. I remember him wearing a string vest one year and when he took it off, its pattern was tanned on his chest and back.

He sometimes used to suck a cherry stone and by the end of the day it was completely white. As there wasn't a fridge in his office, he used to put the milk bottle in a bowl with the tap dripping over it. There were two ladies that used to take the money for tickets: one was Mabel Day, and I only knew the other lady as Flossie, who also worked at the box office at the Cambridge Arts Theatre. Mabel and Pop Day became close friends of Lionel and my mother-in-law, Win, and they used to go on holiday with them – their favourite place being Scotland, but he never did like the sound of bagpipes!

Lionel's main bugbear was getting the balance of the chemicals right, plus all the strange things he used to find in the filters at various times. Before he was custodian at Jesus Green swimming pool (I can't get used to it being called the Lido) he was at Sheep's Green, but I didn't know him then. I really got to know him when I was practising for the swim through Cambridge and he used to let me stay in a bit longer after he blew his whistle.

That was a number of years before I met his son Colin Langford on a blind

> **❝ I remember him wearing a string vest one year and when he took it off, its pattern was tanned on his chest and back**

date. But looking back, I must have seen him as there was always a crowd of us at the pool. I'll always remember Lionel for being a lovely father-in-law and a fantastic grandad.

By Julie Langford

COLIN BECKETT

As a boy, I went to the Manor School in the 1960s and had swimming lessons at Jesus Green Lido.

Lionel was a lovely man and when I was a wimpy young boy I went swimming there and it was so cold.

They used to let the schools go in before it opened, and Lionel said to me, "What's the matter with you?"

I said, "It's f-f-f-freezing!"

He said, "Just a minute," and he went into his office, came out with a kettle and poured some hot water into the swimming pool for me.

"How's that?" he asked.

And I said, "The same, f-f-f-freezing!"

RUTH ECKSTEIN

Ruth Eckstein remembers her grandmother and regular JG swimmer, Dr Erna Eckstein. Aged 100, Ruth attributed her longevity to a boiled egg every morning and a swim.

MY GRANNY WAS in Düsseldorf in 1936 and the family had to get out of Germany. They knew war was coming and my grandad, Dr Albert Eckstein, who was a paediatrician, had applied to various places to get out, including the UK, USA and Turkey. The first visa to turn up was for Turkey, so he

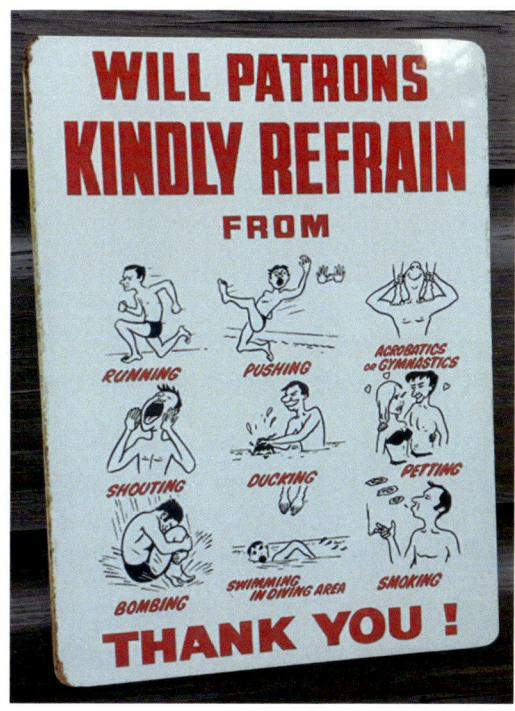

visited Ankara before returning to collect my granny and their three boys, one of whom was my dad.

They had a very happy time in Ankara. There were lots of Jewish refugees who were being kept an eye on, but they had a very good life in Turkey and did a lot of travelling throughout the country.

My granny had always been a swimmer. In Germany she swam in the Baltic, where the coast has those lovely little beach huts. I've got thousands of photos of her in the early 1900s from summer trips at the Baltic Sea with those little wicker Strandkörbe where they'd get changed and lie down to enjoy the sunshine. They were always very Germanic swimmers – very healthy, into fresh air and swimming because it was good for you.

They left Turkey in the 1950s because my granddad got a job in Hamburg. He only lived there for a couple of years because he died of a bee sting, and my granny moved to Cambridge to live with my dad, who was a GP on Arbury Road. He had the surgery built as a new Arbury practice and he built a flat for my granny too.

As soon as she moved to Cambridge, she swam regularly at Jesus Green Pool; almost every day in the summer. In May, she'd be excited about the pool opening and as soon as it opened, she'd be there.

In the 1970s, as soon as we could swim, she'd take us down, me and my brothers. She had a little grey, left-hand drive, German VW Beetle with plastic seats that got so hot in summer that they'd burn your bottom. We always sat at the grassy end of the pool because that's where the sun is in the morning. We swam with her and then we liked to fool around on our own.

After our swim, granny would give us a chocolate button sandwich, but we had to change out of our wet swimming costumes first, which she said caused 'women's problems' later in life. So we'd always have a dry swimming costume to change into because it was very bad to sit with a wet costume on.

In the 1970s, the pool had a poster of rules and regulations illustrated with small cartoons. No dive bombing, no eating, no smoking – and no heavy petting. As I was quite young, that embarrassed me a bit because although I thought it was pretty raunchy, I didn't know what it meant and nobody would ever tell me.

Granny always wore a bikini and a 1960s bathing cap – slightly eccentric, which sometimes embarrassed me a bit. She would always do two lengths of breaststroke, that was her workout! She loved Jesus Green Pool. There was such

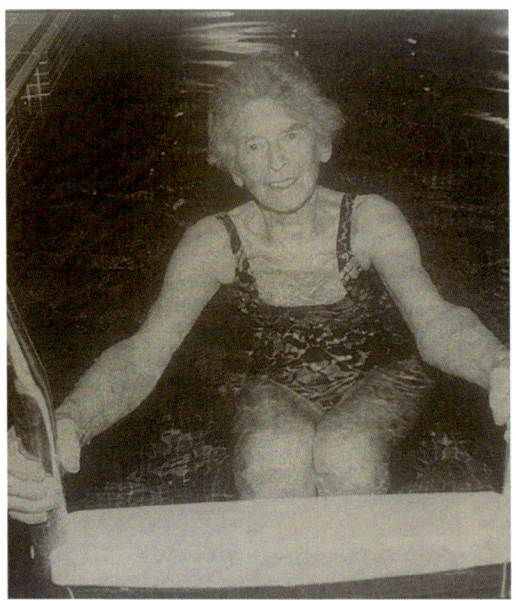

Ruth's granny Dr Erna Eckstein was a Lido fan

camaraderie, she'd meet all her oldie friends and they'd chat. And eventually, she became one of the oldest swimmers at the pool.

Her favourite time to swim was around 11 o'clock. She had a towelling bathrobe – a poncho with a hood – and she slipped her bikini off underneath on poolside; she never used the changing rooms, she loved to be in the open air. She'd always had her chocolate button sandwiches, she'd do a bit of sunbathing and she usually spent a couple of hours at the pool before jumping back into her little grey Beetle and heading home.

She swam until she was 100 but in her last few years she was too frail to pull herself out of the water on the metal bars by the steps. And when people asked her about how she'd lived such a long life, she would always say 'A boiled egg every morning and swimming,' that was her absolute rule for longevity.

TIM VERNEY

Tim Verney worked at Cambridge Evening News. In August 1985, he swam through Cambridge's pools from the Abbey to Parkside and Jesus Green Lido, and in August 2023, he returned to the Lido for its 100th birthday party. Here, he introduces a piece he wrote almost 40 years ago about that eighties swim.

I HAD BEEN a reporter with the *Cambridge Evening News* for two years when I wrote the article. I certainly remember the occasion. It was a fun adventure away from the office, albeit one in which you had to swim for your supper.

I remember it being quite a busy morning, travelling up and down the pools and between them. One thing I recall – as a rather slow swimmer – is that I took a pair of fins to try to speed things up, but I'm not sure I used them.

It's funny to see all the temperatures in the article are in Fahrenheit only (in Celsius for today's reader, on his visit Parkside was at 28.9C and Jesus Green at 17.8C). That, and the fact the Abbey was still an outdoor pool, date the piece. And then there are the wonderful memories from pool veteran Arthur Mansfield, who had been swimming at Jesus Green since soon after it was built, even recalling the men digging out the ground.

More recently, after a swim, I placed my coffee on a solid structure just outside the pool right next to the river – forgetting, as Mr Mansfield had related, that this was where water used to be channelled from river to pool, and back from pool to river. I'll remember in future.

I was so pleased that a visit to the pool last year coincided with the centenary celebrations. I loved the inflatable obstacle course, a star attraction for the day. Stretching into the watery yonder, I just had to test it out, though I think it tackled me as much as I did it. And how lovely to meet some of those who have worked to keep the pool open when its future has been less certain, and whose continued efforts have helped to ensure there was a centenary to celebrate. May there be many more such landmark moments.

I suppose much has changed at the pool over the years, but it's what has not changed that strikes me particularly. The sentinel canopy of trees – forever sparing in the sunlight that they allow through to warm the water; the spartan wooden changing huts with sprinklings of leaves and grit; the scaffolding on the pump room – in place so long you'd be more worried if it weren't there.

And, of course, the magical entrance. As you approach, a break in the long expanse of dark wood reveals a sapphire glimpse of the pool. With old-fashioned turnstiles and a temperature board on whose arrow you pin hopes of a

THE PEOPLE'S POOL

favourable reading, day after day it's a view that still seems to intrigue and delight passers-by who hadn't realised what was there. If their enthusiasm is tempered a little by the realisation the water may not be quite as warm as they would like, I hope they will not be put off and will carry home the story about a partly hidden jewel they discovered.

OUR INTREPID REPORTER TRIES OUT THE WATER
CAMBRIDGE EVENING NEWS, 13 AUGUST 1987

Enough had been written about public swimming pools in Cambridge. It was time to try them out. Word had been filtering through about the charms of Jesus Green. And where on earth was the Abbey Pool? Did you really need a numbered tag at Parkside just to remember who you were among the teeming hundreds? Reporter Tim Verney laid down his pen, and headed for open water with photographer Tony Jedrej.

IT WAS A typical summer's day. The weather, already threatening, looked set to worsen. But there was no avoiding it – Cambridge's three main swimming pools just had to be tested.

In a moment of unthinking enthusiasm I had agreed to take the plunge and swim a length or so in the Abbey, Jesus Green and Parkside pools.

What a shock! The variation in water temperature was 20 degrees Fahrenheit. Indoor Parkside was like bathwater at 84F. But outdoor Jesus Green proved a real flesh chiller at 64F.

But first stop was Abbey, the outdoor pool where the first job of the morning for attendants is to try to remove the frogs which hop into the water from a nearby ditch overnight.

Head attendant Andy Hill, 21, from Histon, explained: "There have been up to half a dozen. The trouble is as soon as you try to scoop them up they dive down to the bottom of the pool."

Having frogmarched them away, the secluded pool, just a stone's throw from

Jesus Green Pool, popular as ever, in 1971

the Cambridge United football ground, is ready for business.

Nervously I descended the ladder into the three-foot shallow end. Agony. Mr Hill was adamant that the temperature rarely falls below 70F thanks to heating, but it felt like freshly melted ice.

Children on a summer play scheme splashed about with inflatable toys. I headed the 50 yards along to the deep end, passing pensioner Phyllis Horne, of Mill End Road, Cherry Hinton – an ardent supporter of the pool – on the way.

Ramshackle timber buildings surround the water, the changing room is a bench behind a hut and the only sign of modernisation I saw was council painter Roy Mainwaring giving a light blue lick to the paintwork.

Yet there is something peaceful about the Abbey pool – a friendly, hidden jewel few know is there. And you can park.

As a plane buzzed into the air from nearby Marshall's Airport I completed a second length – immune to the cold now – then jumped out and headed for Jesus Green.

There was an air of surrealism. Not a soul was in the 100-yard-long pool, which looked still and inviting despite being unheated.

I brushed some leaves out of the way and set off on a length of backstroke. Progress was slow. The pool is one of the longest in the country – only 18 lengths and you have swum a mile.

Numerous stories abound. A few weeks ago, a mother and her four ducklings took a swim. The bathe over, mum hopped out and waddled away when she realised her brood could not manage the jump. Staff had to remove one of the diving boards and create a ramp so they could walk out.

Then there is the tale of a colleague who, rather short-sighted without his glasses, bade a polite good morning to what he thought was a rare occurrence, another swimmer in the pool at the same time. When he emerged from the water he discovered his pool-mate was in fact a plastic football.

But that is indicative of the esteem in which devotees hold Jesus Green. It may only have 20 to 30 swimmers a day, but they are real regulars, including a 94-year-old woman. The oldest diver is an 82-year-old woman.

I managed one length, zigzagging backwards from side to side as if trying to avoid an imaginary torpedo attack.

The marvellous thing about these outdoor pools is that the chlorine does not get up your nose. And you become immune to the cold after a while. The colder the water, the warmer the air feels afterwards.

Attendant Dean Gregory, 25, bemoaned the fact that too many people pass by the beautifully screened pool, flanked by tall trees on one side and pre-war wooden changing huts on the other.

"It's such a good facility and there's a great atmosphere. It needs more advertising, people don't know it's here. When I lived nearby, I used to pass it every day and did not realise it was here.

"It opened up for the season in May with a temperature of 57F. High point was our last really hot weekend when the water temperature rose to 78F and 2,000 passed through the turnstiles."

As I clambered out, one of the pool's veterans made one of his almost daily appearances – 77-year-old Arthur Mansfield of Kimberley Road.

Rain or shine he ploughs a quarter of a mile through the water most days. He has been swimming there regularly since 1923, soon after the pool was finished. We managed to halt him just as he was about to do another length at fast crawl pace.

"I feel like Rothschild in here," he declared proudly, surveying the expanse of water around.

He recalled the pool in its earliest days. "I remember it being dug out after the First World War. The men went on strike for a farthing an hour more and were all sacked.

"The water was channelled straight from the river – you can still see where. When it got dirty, it was channelled back into the river and new water was brought in. The river water was so fresh then you could drink it. In those days the pool was surrounded by grass."

The former railway signalman said he was taking it easy because of a cold. But he showed no sign of it as he launched into another length.

Like Abbey, Jesus Green pool is another hidden gem, a landscaped haven of cool charm, sadly neglected by a warm-water-seeking public.

Final port of call was where nearly everybody goes. Follow the smell of chlorine and you come to Parkside Pool.

The two lengths I swam here may have been in the hottest water temperature of the day, but they were anything but enjoyable.

When the pool is full – and it nearly always seems to be – backstroke is hazardous. It is a bit like sailing into the Gulf without a minesweeper to protect you.

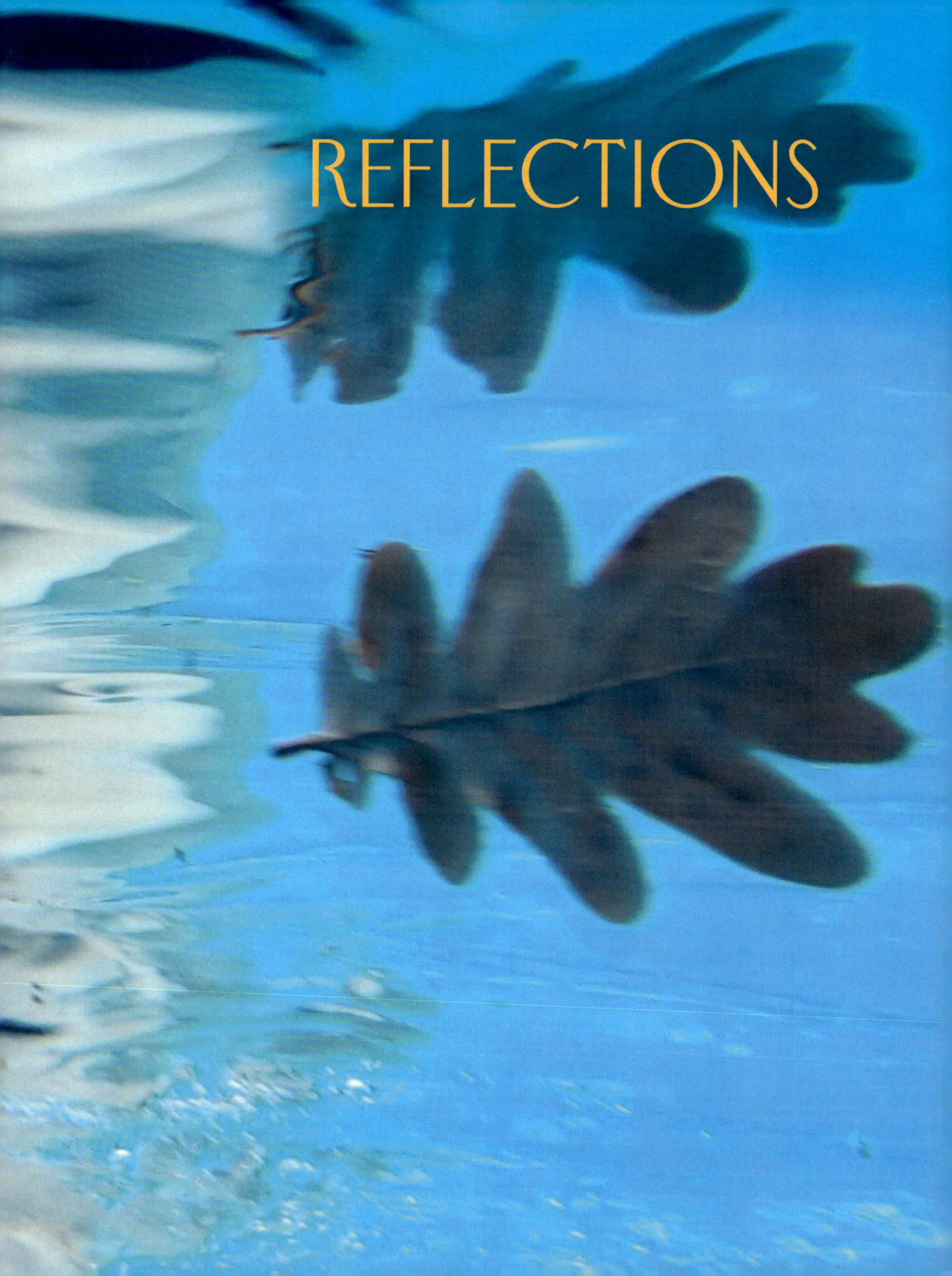

ANNE GARVEY

JESUS GREEN LIDO is a centrepiece in my life. Since the first day I clapped eyes on its fabulous slinky length and bosky, fronded surrounds, I was a devotee. I might have taken dedication too far on a cold bleak snowy January Saturday night, when I set off for Francis Jeans' fancy dress winter pool party, dressed in not much more than a green swimsuit, natural fishnet tights, eight-inch heels and a sash. Yes, I was Miss Jesus Green – luckily the winner, and it was worth the chill.

Over the years Jesus Green has been a meeting place, a centre of aquatic contemplation, a balm in times of grief. My test for its healing properties went like this. In a terrible fix? Go to one end of the pool and assess your mood; if low and depressed, own it. Then swim a couple of lengths, go to the same spot and reassess. Invariably and reliably you feel better.

My children all swam happily at Jesus Green and now grandchildren love it; they spend longer in the warm-up shower than in the pool, but it's great fun.

I think my lowest point at Jesus Green – literally – was one perfect sunny day in June. I had swum, changed and was on my way home, sporting my latest Vivienne Westwood sundress, a great swim bag, high heels (again) and sunglasses. These might have been a bit too dark, for I suddenly heard a huge splash and actually realised in two seconds I was at the very bottom of the deep end. My lodger, who was watching amazed from the other side of the pool, remarked, 'I thought you were going to stop walking, Annie, but no!'

Jesus Green has had its lows too – the bright idea of enlisting the Army from Waterbeach barracks to terrorise swimmers with military discipline one season, possibly the worst – but today its sunny management and debonaire supervisor, along with the ever-wry and fun Mary and a team of affable gals and chaps create a fabulous atmosphere that's frankly hard to match anywhere.

BRONWEN DINNEEN

A Jesus Green regular since 1987, Bronwen is usually in blue: blue hat, blue swimsuit, blue towel, arriving late, getting waylaid by friends and conversation, always saying, "I must get into the water."

I DIP MY hand into the pool right in the centre at the deepest section and dream of:

That long narrow rectangle of blue, first spotted on my Cambridge map in 1987.

My son, at the age of 9 months, taking his first plunges – Humpty Dumpty, Round and Round.

The garden – floating on bright orange armbands on a sunny August afternoon.

Water painting, with buckets and brushes on the sunny slope.

Conversations with a cricket-and train-enthusiast on the top bench.

The ever-changing but always welcoming team of friendly lifeguards. Getting to know them and wishing them well as they moved on to new adventures.

Long, relaxing evenings swimming and sunning ourselves until the diminishing rays sent us all squeezing into the top corner of the slope.

The comfort of knowing that there would always be friends to chat to and laugh with, especially during challenging times.

My son, a regular lido enthusiast, diving in and completing lengths with determination – mainly underwater.

Patterns made by swirling September leaves – gold and bronze against the deep blue.

Wood pigeons balancing on the steps, and taking a drink in the peace of the evening when most people had left.

The memorable afternoon two days after the Brexit result when thunder and hail arrived with a vengeance and steam rose up from the surface of the water. Walking over hailstones to reach the sauna.

The poignant evenings in September as the pool closed for the winter, then meeting friends in late January and commenting that we only had three and a half months until opening day!

JOAN LUDMAN

From competition to contemplation, Jesus Green Lido is home for Joan Ludman.

I HAVE BEEN swimming at Jesus Green Pool for probably 70 years. When we first came here there were no showers, and the diving boards were near the entrance, and there was just one head caretaker and there were no lifeguards – there was just Ted the caretaker.

Ted taught me to swim. He was the swimming teacher, caretaker, basket man, cleaner, lifeguard, and took the money. He did all that on his own. He used a ring on the end of a pole to teach swimming.

The pool is an escape from everything else that goes on in your life, it's an oasis, it's a calming oasis. Often in life there are things that worry you and you feel a bit uptight and you come here and have a swim and the cares seem to float away in the water. You definitely feel a bit better when you come out, even if you are a bit hesitant and the water is a bit cold when you go in, it is always worth it once you've had your swim.

I love everything about Jesus Green Pool – I like the social aspect but I just love watching the people going up and down the pool, I just love everything about it really. The pool gives me a sense of peace and I don't know what I'd do without it – I can't imagine it and don't want to think about it.

I much prefer to swim outdoors but I do swim indoors in the winter because I know myself, I couldn't cope with the really cold water, but I am quite relieved when I can come back to Jesus Green. I think it is a brilliant idea to have the pool open all year because lots of people do love cold water swimming, and I was able to come back in April rather than May because of the extended opening.

The community is special here – you are accepted whatever and whoever – there is no judgement. You are who you are, and we know who everyone is.

I used to swim competitively, I used to be a fairly good swimmer and now I am old, I just plod, a comfortable plodding swimmer. I front crawl. I started competing when I was 10 or 11. I swam for Granta Swimming Club. I did all events from individual medley to back crawl – backstroke was my best event. I did long distances and short distances. I did most things. My father had been a keen swimmer and water polo player and he

DAVID FIRMAN

I have swum in many places over the years, from thousands of miles in swimming pools to the turquoise waters of the Pacific, other oceans, seas, lakes and rivers. Swimming my first lengths of Jesus Green, I had no thought that four decades later this would be my favourite place to swim almost every day.

On hot days, a dip in the cool water is wonderful, as is swimming in the pouring rain. Basking in autumn sunshine is such a glorious feeling and a swim on a freezing overcast February morning is exhilarating. All these swims have been a joy!

was the one who introduced us to Jesus Green pool and encouraged us, whereas my mother wouldn't even dip her toe in.

My father was born in 1911 and he remembered Jesus Green Pool being built and filled with river water. When I was young, I used to do all my training at Jesus Green Pool, and I used to do quite a lot of pleasure and leisure here, but the river was important for the Granta Swimming Club community.

Jesus Green was a great facility which complemented the river swimming. We could train for our river events, such as the swim through Cambridge. We trained at Jesus Green in the morning before school. I used to do 10 lengths, go home and have breakfast and go to school.

After school we went to the pool for pleasure. I remember doing a back dive on the 5m diving board and I suddenly caught sight of a bird out of the corner of my eye, and I lost my concentration and did a belly flop.

When I was a pupil at Chesterton, I used to bring the first-year pupils down to the pool with the swimming teacher to help her. I was already competing myself then. Her name was Miss Lloyd and she'd always ask me to come and help which I loved, and I missed maths (which I was rubbish at). We had some competitions at the pool, and we had a gala where we used to dress up as clowns and go off the diving boards.

Most of the competitions were in the river. I won the through-Cambridge swim, all three distances – the half mile, the mile, and the two-and-a-quarter miles. I liked distances then. I continued racing until I was 20 or 21 and then I got married and I think I out-pooled myself.

I didn't want to see another pool until I started taking the children.

Swimming became important again for me later in life. Someone at the school I worked at challenged me to a race, so I thought I should start training. I started going to the Abbey, but it was a bit hit-and-miss because of lessons so I went to Jesus Green, and I thought, "Oh my goodness, I am home. This is where I should be." You know when you walk in somewhere and you think, "This is where I belong." So, from then on, I became a regular and that's about 20 years ago. The lifeguards now are very helpful, and you can't fault them.

I love to sit in the same place. I like to

" The community is special here – you are accepted whatever and whoever – there is no judgement

sit at the bottom end of the pool by the ladies' changing rooms and when I have finished my swim, I can grab my bag and go straight in the shower – it's a practical routine. I love sitting here watching the trees and as the summer progresses the leaves change colour and begin to fall into the water. I also just love to watch the swimmers and things around the pool.

Sitting here, you would never think you were in the centre of the city. Anything that's going on in Cambridge is not part of it. It's so totally different.

Jassy Marshall with friends Hannah Scott, left, and Julie Verrechia, right

JASSY MARSHALL

GROWING UP IN Cambridge, Jesus Green Lido was always referred to as 'the pool'. I went to Park Street school and a group of us would go straight from school. Back then in the late 1970s and 80s it felt like it was more a pool for the kids. There was a green springboard and two diving boards. We would bomb, belly flop and dive for hours. Where the sauna is now was a large tuck shop – opening onto Jesus Green as well as the pool – which sold sweets.

We had an arrangement with the lifeguards that if we collected all the clothes baskets from around the pool, we'd get a free entry ticket for the next day. It was a perfect arrangement.

In my late teens I must confess it was quite common to go for a midnight swim. We'd climb in at the men's end, and you'd always bump into someone you knew. It was exciting at the time but in hindsight probably not the best idea.

Now, in my middle age, I have discovered the joys of cold water swimming.

Jesus Green is a unique gem of a community in Cambridge, a melting pot of all walks of life and ages, bound together by the pure joy of escaping the trappings of daily life for a moment and swimming among the trees, listening to the birds, and just being.

MARY WILLIAMS

Mary Williams, or Smiley Mary as she's known to other swimmers, talks knitted swimming trunks, artists and the healing powers of the Lido.

PEOPLE CALL ME Smiley Mary. The pool just makes me smile. And everyone else. It's such a relaxing place. It's the whole ambience here – the trees, the people, the whole place. If you could bottle it, I always say you'd be a multi-millionaire.

I call it Jesus Green Pool rather than the Lido. Lidos are grander and some of our lidos are so beautiful. But there's nowhere like Jesus Green Pool with our lovely lime trees. Other outdoor pools might have beautiful buildings but we've got the most beautiful surroundings.

I learned to swim here – and at the Abbey when it was an open-air pool – when I was seven or eight. I came here with my three children when they were teenagers. And then I started coming on my own. I've been coming here on my own for about 35 years.

So many people come here on their own. It's lovely when people come with partners and families, but it's a place you can come on your own and relax. When I started coming I was greeted by a lady called May Meadows. And you still get that sort of greeting when you walk through the gate today. It's irreplaceable.

May was a delight and she was my welcoming committee. She used to come here on her own but she'd have swum here with her children when the pool first opened. She had twin daughters. They were in the swimming club and were really good swimmers.

May used to sit up near where the heaters are now. She'd say, "Come and sit down," and then she said, "This is a happy place. You can make it happy by simply saying hello to somebody every day." And that's true, isn't it? That was 35 years ago and we're still carrying on her legacy.

I've always had people talk to me and my daughter's the same. There are just some people you can open up to. People have sat with me and told me about a bereavement, the loss of a child, terrible things. I think being outside helps people relax, and when they feel comfortable they can open up to whoever happens to be near. If we could see all the problems

that people leave on the bottom of the pool we'd be in for a shock, because people come here with really big problems.

Lots of artists come here. They'd send me postcards they'd painted here or pictures of the pool. That used to help me through the winter. When it used to close I'd go into complete withdrawal. My husband used to have to take me away that weekend. There's nothing else that quite ticks all the boxes. It's very special.

Last year I swam until the end of November and came back in April. I got down to about 7 or 8 degrees. I didn't like putting on all the gear – the gloves and booties – but I still loved it. You get hooked don't you? Now I love it just as much in winter as the summer. All this beautiful array of changing robes. You see them pedalling like mad down Huntingdon Road in their robes – I've even seen leopard print ones – the robes are just as diverse as the swimmers.

I recently swam indoors for the first time but there's no comparison. Being outdoors makes all the difference. We're all outdoor creatures by nature and we know how good nature is for us, just being outside, seeing the trees and hearing the birdsong. And no two days are ever the same – the people, the atmosphere. You can sit here at seven o'clock in the evening and watch the sunset or see the sunrise in the morning. It's always different.

I've got arthritic knees so they've told me not to do breaststroke and I never learned front crawl. So I can only do backstroke now, but that means I can see more of the sky and the clouds.

I don't have a routine here. I don't do

routines with anything in my life, I don't wear watches, since I retired. Life's too short to spend it doing things that I don't want to do. I don't sit at the men's end very often. It's too smelly. It's not their fault, it's where the canal boats empty their loos. But I wonder how the men can eat their sandwiches down there on certain days! We tend to gather at the other end and when the men come down here they say they're coming to the women's end. I think that's hilarious because nothing is really men's or women's here now.

Swimmers I remember are Gus and Vangelina. Gus Siddle wore woollen swimming trunks that his wife knitted for him. They were blue or white and a very fine knit. They survived the water but I don't know how comfortable they were – I never asked him that.

Vangelina (Evangeline Thorgerson, née Collier) I got to know in her 80s and 90s, but she'd swum here for many years and had such stories to tell. Some people used to hide from Vangelina, but I was drawn to her. She went to Summerhill School so she'd grown up without rules. It made her who she was. She was very artistic, a potter, and had such an interesting life. She'd think nothing of getting on any form of transport and travelling anywhere in the world on her own. Her son Storm Thorgerson did the cover art for Pink Floyd.

We've had so many wonderful people here – and we still do, don't we?

I've never seen anybody come in and look worse when they go out. I think that would be impossible. I can't think of anywhere else that you get such a nice welcome.

PHILIP BOULDING KC

From 'basket boy' to head lifeguard while a student at the University, Philip Boulding can't believe how lucky he was to work at Jesus Green.

I HAD THE pleasure and the privilege of working at the UK's longest swimming pool back in the 1970s when, as a result of a contact made with the Parkside pool manager, Brian Allison, when swimming for both the Cambridge and Granta amateur swimming clubs, I was given a job at Jesus Green pool during the summer of my gap year before going to the University of Cambridge.

The year in question was 1972 and I worked as a 'basket boy' under the then head lifeguard, the formidable Lionel Langford who was – principally through his long service at Jesus Green pool – very much a Cambridge character. Lionel was also renowned for his very distinguished war record in the WWII battles against the Japanese.

In those days the pool opened on 1 May and closed on 31 September each year. It opened at 7am every day and would stay open until 9pm unless the weather was poor, in which case it would close at 7pm (save on Sunday as I recall, when it would always close at 7pm). It was a long, but very pleasurable day!

The job of the basket boy was principally to take care of the baskets into which swimmers deposited their clothes and to hand them back to the swimmers once they had finished swimming. Obviously, the intensity of the work was heavily dependent on the weather and whilst on a poor weather day there was at 7am, the first of three daily checks of pool water temperature would take place. A temperature of 70F (21C) was a real cause for celebration! However, the pool temperature regularly failed to exceed 66 or 67F. Swimming in such relatively low temperatures was an exhilarating experience, which is now a regular pastime among wild swimmers.

After my 1972 summer as the basket boy, I was re-engaged for each of the summers of 1973 through to 1977 as the head lifeguard. Given that the University terms did not start until early October each year, and I was available after the Tripos exams which were usually over by the third week of May, I was almost a perfect match for the job.

The head lifeguard's responsibilities were, to say the least, diverse! It was certainly not a case of just assisting swimmers who got into difficulties in the water. In addition, and given the pool's attractiveness to certain loutish elements, particularly on hot days when there were lots of pretty young female swimmers, the head lifeguard on occasion needed to have the qualities of a good nightclub bouncer. Fortunately, being in the Varsity 1st rugby XV, I was quite large!

The head lifeguard also had very important functions in terms of keeping the water in Jesus Green pool in pristine condition. This was because whilst there was a maintenance team for the Cambridge outdoor pools based at the Parkside pool (Les, Gordon and Roger, the latter also being a very well-known DJ in Cambridge in the 70s and 80s with his disco 'Pink Marble'), their time was stretched to say the least. In practice this meant that the head lifeguard had to take a very hands-on role in helping keep the water in the pool in as near perfect condition as possible.

Keeping the water in pristine condition involved regularly back-washing the filter baskets located in the plant room at the very popular sunbathing end of the pool, as well as changing the chlorine gas cylinders which were used to chlorinate the pool. The latter job was particularly tricky given the size and weight of the yellow metal canisters and it was virtually impossible to do it without getting a good whiff of the chlorine – a gas which

> **A temperature of 70F (21C) was a real cause for celebration!**

was particularly toxic as evidenced by the fact that it was used illegally as a weapon by the Germans in the trench warfare during WWI.

Goodness knows what health and safety would make now of this aspect of the then-head lifeguard's job.

Looking back on my time at Jesus Green Pool, I often have to pinch myself to believe I really had the privilege of working there over the course of several summers in the 70s – including the fantastic, never-ending summer of '76. I also had the privilege of making numerous, enduring friendships with the regulars – some of which have lasted to this day. It really is difficult to comprehend just how fortunate I was – not to mention the occasional 'private' swims I had once I had closed the pool for the day to the public.

Saul, third from left, with friends from North Bondi Surf Life Saving Club, including Olympian and world record holder Murray Rose, second from left

SAUL BETMEAD DE CHASTEIGNER

Saul was captain of the North Bondi Surf Life Saving Club (2005–2009), New South Wales Lifesaver of the Year 2003, Sydney Champion Lifesaver 2002/3/4. In 2008, he received a personal commendation from Kevin Rudd, Prime Minister of Australia for contributions to the surf lifesaving movement and the community.

SOME OF MY earliest memories are from Jesus Green. I learned to swim properly there and remember my father Jon swimming with me to the deep end, which weirdly is in the middle, and explaining that swimming was just like flying – you glide over the surface like a bird flies through the sky. The image has stayed with me ever since: throughout the thousands of kilometres I have swum, all over the world, whenever I swim, I always remember that idea and I always remember this pool.

I once told my friend, the late Murray Rose – Olympian and father of the modern freestyle stroke – about the notion that swimming is like flying. He looked at me and said, "What a lovely idea, that's exactly what it should feel like."

Another memory is from a little later. My mother Gill often used to pick up my brother Dominic and I from school and go straight to the pool. There used to be diving boards in the middle of the pool and I was always amazed when my father went to the top board, walked to the edge, then slowly did a handstand, held it for what felt like an eternity and then slowly pushed off into a dive straight down. I don't think anyone else could do it, certainly none of our friends' parents. I have tried many times, but never quite managed it.

From left to right: Lynn Morgan (nee Beavis), Hilary Winfield-Chislett and Alison Winfield-Chislett at Jesus Green Lido around 1962

LYNN MORGAN

I AM HEADING towards my 70s and was born and brought up in Cambridge, where I have lived all my life. Somehow Jesus Green has always been there, although it was never known to us as 'the Lido'.

My earliest recollections are going there with my older sister, my younger brother and my mother, in the school holidays. My mother was able to put my brother in the pushchair, me on the mudguard and all the kit needed for the day draped or shoved in any available space on the pushchair.

Once at the pool my mother would set up camp, laying out towels and bags. Always the end next to the plant room, where the concrete surface sloped down towards the pool. It was invariably the sunnier end, albeit the concrete could be quite unforgiving.

Long before I could reach the bottom of the shallow ends, I would hang on for dear life to the sides and try to swim around the steps – my mother tells me this is how I indeed learned to swim. My younger brother would jump recklessly from the side, relying on my mother to grab him in time to stop him actually drowning.

Later there were of course the weekly swimming lessons. From Brunswick School, it was an easily walkable distance. I don't remember too much of those lessons, I may have wiped them from my memory for self-preservation as I remember it always being cold and grey. I did, however, get my 14-yard swimming certificate which was a rare success in my younger life.

One of the benefits of being able to swim was that I was allowed to go to Jesus Green with my best friend and her older sister. I was still at junior school but can remember idling away hours at the pool and trying out the diving board – in those days parents were more relaxed about children disappearing for the day. Of course the snack bar was a huge draw, although as it was open both poolside and to Jesus Green itself, queues would often build up on both sides. This meant that even on a warm day, you ended up shivering until you were finally served.

About this time my father would sometimes take us three children to the pool on a Sunday morning. Interestingly, my memories of those outings were that it was always sunny. This is undoubtedly because my father's raison d'être was to earn brownie points for taking us out whilst my mother cooked Sunday lunch. He could also pass a pleasant hour or two reading the Sunday papers in the sun, catching up with friends, all with just a casual glance to see if all three children were still alive. The image of maroon knitted men's bathing trunks still haunts me: unflattering when they were dry, hideous when they were wet. As he was quite a stylish man throughout his life, I can only think these were sartorially acceptable in the late 60s and early 70s.

I don't think swimming featured much in my teenage years and early twenties, I probably went to the new pool (aka Parkside). Certainly we went there for school swimming lessons, thank God, but at the time I certainly didn't regard swimming as cool.

By the time my own children arrived, I think I had managed to reframe my childhood excursions to Jesus Green pool with a rosy hue which I was always trying to recreate with them. There were certainly picnics with friends and other families which were actually fun, but I think if I were to ask my sons about it they would remember it as being cold and uncomfortable. It will be interesting to see whether my grandchildren are made of sturdier stuff.

ROSIE TWEEN

Rosie sadly died earlier this year. This contribution is an extract of the Cambridge Curiosity and Imagination Taking Note project, where members of the Addenbrooke's community were invited to take note of a moment of happiness in their lives.

SWIMMING WAS ONE of the first things I did when I came home on weekend leave from Stoke Mandeville. I had to be there to learn how to cope without the use of my legs. It was summer two years ago. We would make a picnic and go down to Jesus Green pool on the Saturday. It made me feel things were still possible. I had said straight after the accident that I wasn't going to give up these things though it was totally different swimming without any legs.

I first started swimming regularly when I was working as a nurse in Australia. I would start at 7 and finish at 3 and be knackered and swimming would totally revive me. It does revive me now, but mostly when I swim I feel this immense sense of satisfaction and pleasure. Jesus Green Pool offers me a community. I love going down there, coming in and seeing that clear blue water and the trees and the smiley lifeguards. You always meet somebody you know and even if you don't know them they will say hello. There's something about swimming outside because you're in touch with nature – you can see the sky and the trees. It's very special. That feeling of water and gliding through – I love it.

www.cambridgecandi.org.uk/index.php/our-work/communities/taking-note

RUTH BARNETT

Ruth Barnett learned to swim at Jesus Green 70 years ago. In childhood it was the garden she didn't have at home. She shares her regular routine, reflects on how little the Lido has changed, and names her favourite lifeguard.

I FIRST CAME to Jesus Green Pool about 70 years ago with my mum and brother Martin, who was a toddler then. I came to learn to swim but never remember mum going in the water. Dad only came once, in the 1950s. Ted, the lifeguard and custodian gave him a tour of the plant room, including the new filtration system, which would keep hair out of the pool and keep the water clean.

Ted wore long, white trousers and a white T-shirt. He taught us to swim using a ring at the end of a pole. One day he'd take the ring off and you'd suddenly be able to swim. I don't know how he knew when the moment was right, but it was a miracle. Learning to swim was like riding a bike, that feeling of achievement; suddenly I could do it – swim!

We were given swimming certificates when we were young – for 14 yards, 25 yards and 100 yards. We were so proud of our achievements. Now, when I bring my grandson and he has to swim a certain distance to get a wristband, it's the same kind of joy on his face.

There used to be two springboards on either side of three static boards opposite the entrance. I was always too scared to go off the top board because I thought I'd hit my head. Apart from that there haven't been many changes over time, and I like that, I like that it's a bit scruffy, I like the leaves in the pool and the cobwebs in the changing rooms, but I'm glad we have showers now.

The sauna I'm ambivalent about. It's where there used to be a kiosk which served Jesus Green as well as the pool. It sold sweets – you could get eight fruit salads for an old penny.

We had lunch at the pool every day in summer and would bring our own food. Mum would collect us – me, my brother, and our friends Janet and Richard from Milton Road primary school, take us to the pool for lunch and a swim, and then take us back to school. She'd come and get us again after school and we'd return to the pool for the afternoon.

We had a season ticket and were at the pool all the time. Nigel, another friend, remembers running to Jesus Green pool at the beginning of the season to get the first season ticket. They were numbered, and he wanted number one but he usually only managed to get number two or three.

We didn't have a garden when we were young. Richard and Janet didn't have a garden either. Jesus Green was like our garden and it felt like our own private pool. When it's quiet, it still does.

Jesus Green pool feels as idyllic now as it felt then. It's my favourite place on earth – and I've been to a lot of places in the world. It's a perfect place, it's paradise. I love the water, I love the social bit of it, it's peaceful, I love the trees.

The pool calms me down if I am feeling anxious, it makes me happy and I'm so pleased it's open in the winter now, although I am not a regular winter swimmer. I feel really protective of Jesus Green. I feel it's our pool and I'm very

proud of it. And when I hear people chatting who've travelled some distance to get here I realise we're so lucky to have it.

We have a special swimming pool community, a Jesus Green community. When I came back to Cambridge 20 years ago after having been away for quite a few years, I would bring my book. Now, when I bring my book, I never get round to reading it because there is always someone to chat to.

It is a democratic place, and the management usually listen to our ideas, hence yoga classes and tai chi. It's such a beautiful setting for exercise with the sounds and the sights. I've also volunteered to sweep up leaves and paint the bins at the beginning of the season with other regulars.

When I first learned to swim it was breaststroke. Joan Ludman and I were in the Granta Swimming Club and I'd compete in backstroke and breaststroke. I learned front crawl and tumble turns in my 40s. Tumble turns give me labyrinthitis so I don't do them any more. I still do front crawl for exercise but I do breaststroke too because I like looking at the sky, the trees and the people.

My routine is always the same. I put on my swimming costume before I come so that I can get in quickly. If I'm first in the queue I have to be first in the pool. When you're first in the water the surface is calm and your swimming makes beautiful ripples. In the summer, I try not to use my towel. I drive to a friend's house in Chesterton and cycle from there. On the way back home I always put my towel and swimming costume on the dashboard to dry out in the sunshine.

The lifeguards are wonderful. Every season we get different ones and every season they're so lovely. Sometimes they return and it's lovely to see them again. George was a particular favourite because he always called me by my name. If I needed to be rescued from the water, I'd love to be saved by them!

STEVE TUNNICLIFFE-WILSON
JUST AFTER FOUR

It's just after four
I'm first in
The sun sets
behind the trees
The water is still
I glide gently through it
Listening to the sounds
Of waves slapping gently
On old concrete walls
Clack-clack from the skate park
And herbal smells
Ducks land in the corner
No one in the fast lane yet
But then they arrive
Young men in neoprene
Ladies in their cossies
A few quick lengths
Then up the stairs
Into a robe
Scuttle to the sauna
Spring brings green
Grass grows on the banks
Then flowers
A Turneresque white smear
in the grey sky
Shimmering off the surface
Temperatures rise
More arrive
Isn't it cold?
Not like February
Then warmer still
Wetsuits discarded
Like winter plumage
Embracing the water
Intimately
No longer afraid
Leaves above
Then children everywhere
Splashing furiously
Shrieking with joy
A grandfather watches
Perhaps remembering
His own time
In this
Watery playground
Summer ends
Back to school
Quieter now
Gradually cooling
Leaves falling
First on the water
Then down to the bottom
Twigs in the face
But we don't care
Isn't it lovely?
Do you come every day?
How far do you swim?
Are you a member?
How much were those gloves?
So nice that it's sunny!
Thumbs are freezing
Cramp in the calves
My mile is done
Climbing the steps
Change on the bench
Into my clothes
Dry at last
Slowly warming
Invigorated
Restored
Mind and body
Cleansed together
And thankful
For an old pool

SUE ROGERS
WHAT JESUS GREEN LIDO MEANS TO ME

It's summer 2020
I'm peering through the fence.
The pool is sad and empty
To go home is a wrench.
But wait! One day there's action
The clean-up has begun!
The season's short and strict
But we manage to have fun.
Next spring we're swimming early
They're starting a new trend
And we can't believe our luck
When the season doesn't end.
The winter chill does grip us
Are we mad? Have we no fear?
Then the sun shines on the bench
And we know just why we're here.
For me, the Lido's magic.
It makes my spirits soar
And the people are terrific
I couldn't ask for more
(well, maybe Fridays and Saturdays in
   winter?!)

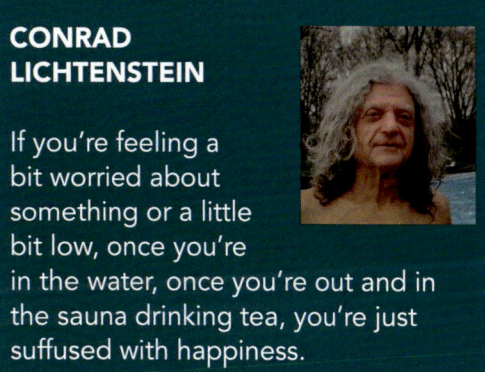

CONRAD LICHTENSTEIN

If you're feeling a bit worried about something or a little bit low, once you're in the water, once you're out and in the sauna drinking tea, you're just suffused with happiness.

Winter folk

ANNA-ROSE HARRIS

Anna-Rose Harris resolved to swim a mile in cold water during her – and the Lido's – first year of winter swimming. Here, she explains how it's helped her manage chronic pain and boosted her self-confidence, and says what makes Jesus Green a little corner of paradise.

IT'S JUST BEAUTIFUL here today, really glorious. It's because it's February and the sun's shining. The water is still quite cold, but I like it when it's 6C or under. Halfway through my second length I always turn onto my back. I look up and it feels like I'm in paradise because it's so bright and blue.

A winter swim for me is normally 12 lengths, and if the water's below 5C then I drop down to 10 lengths. When I started last winter I thought I'd do one length per degree C, but then I met Pilvi in the sauna. They're amazing. They do something like 20 lengths in winter. So I just decided to do 10 lengths every time; that's what I did last year and this year a bit more.

When it gets below 8C I put on boots and gloves. I normally swim with just a bobble hat but I've had to wear a neoprene cap as well because I've just had my hair cut really short. It's a lot warmer than you'd think, your hair.

I'm not new to swimming but I've discovered I'm a cold water swimmer. At school, I was always in the bottom set of swimming because of asthma. But I also swam with my mum in the summer, she's a massive swimmer. But then I kind of just stopped.

When I developed chronic migraine, I started swimming again for the cold water. I'd read it was helpful for pain. So I started swimming in the River Cam and it was amazing; my pain would just disappear.

My migraine is exercise induced. When it first became chronic, it would take me about 10 minutes to get up a flight of stairs because my head would pound so much. I kept telling myself that I should be fitter, I should be able to swim a whole length. When I did, I'd swim too fast and then be incapacitated for days. So I had

HAMRA YUCEL

Losing my mother during Lockdown and not being able to attend her funeral had been tough to say the least, but losing connection to friends and normal activities made my grief even harder to overcome.

Then my husband and I started swimming at the Lido in May 2021. Neither of us had previous experience of swimming in water colder than 17C and were not sure how long we'd carry on in the winter months. We have not only exceeded our own expectations, but in our late 50s also discovered new strengths we did not know we had. Now, we swim five days a week at temperatures as low as 3.6C.

Cold water swimming and finding a like-minded community helped me get through a very challenging time. Now I'd feel incomplete if I did not start the day with a swim.

to do less, just doing half a length or swimming really slowly.

What really helped was coming swimming with my then girlfriend, now wife. She's really shortsighted but obviously takes her glasses off to swim, so I'm her guide swimmer. And we'd swim really slowly because she's not really a swimmer. That really helped me slow down: instead of beating myself up about swimming fast and doing exercise, it became about enjoying the water and enjoying being outside.

One summer, when I first started swimming here about five years ago, I brought my mum to Jesus Green. Her granny lived in Cambridge, so she'd come here when she was tiny but didn't remember that until we got here. She remembered the changing rooms and the really long pool. We had a great swim together, and it was really nice to bring her because swimming is what we do together.

When Jesus Green was only open from May to September, I would swim but didn't really know anyone. Winter

opening has changed that. I really feel that this is my community now; I really feel part of the place. I'm a shy person but I really wanted to talk to people. I had to count to 10 in my head and take a deep breath before I'd start a conversation with someone but now chatting to people is the part I love most.

I always speak to someone when I come here, and it's the winter swimming that's transformed it. That's because it's such a shared experience. I always say the hardest part is just getting in. And so whether you've just got in and out, or swum loads of lengths, you have that in common with everyone. In the summer, people are here for fun or for exercise, but in winter there's no room for ego. We're all here for the experience.

In winter, because the hours are compressed, you see the same people every day. And you get to know people chatting in the sauna. Warming up there afterwards always feels amazing, a bit like being drunk and wanting to just chat to everyone. It's really joyful. Even on days when I'm not having a good time, I'll just get myself to the pool and afterwards I will always feel better. You just feel transformed.

And even with my pain, I know that with cold water swimming I'll feel better afterwards. I'm still trying to find the balance. I push myself too hard in the summer. In the winter it's easier because the cold helps you find that balance between effort and ease. This pool is so long that you get into such a rhythm, a meditative state in the water. I feel more at home in the pool than out of it. Every day, it's like, "when am I going to swim?" It's when I feel like myself.

I have really bad social anxiety and find it really hard to talk to people. It's just lack of confidence. It was in the sauna that I was brave, and just started talking. With the cold water and then the sauna, the tension just goes away and you make really warm friends. It's really helped with my confidence. I always wanted to be the type of person who could smile at a stranger in the street, and the only reason I couldn't was lack of confidence. Here, I smile at everyone. Everyone is full of love, I think, for the pool.

I can't swim indoors anymore. It's a pain thing. Indoors, everything is noisy; it's too warm. The chlorine is too strong and there's nothing to do but think about your swimming. Indoors I can get into a very self-critical headspace – I think I should be swimming harder and faster. When you're outside in the cold, it's all about experiencing the water.

Jesus Green Lido is a really special community. It's a special place, a special pool, and it's been the winter swimming here that's transformed me. On New Year's Day 2022 there was a lady who swam a mile, so I wrote in my notebook that my goal was to swim a mile. That was last year and I swam a mile. Then I swam 5km. Then I swam 7km. And that was all down to cold-water swimming – instead of beating myself up about swimming fast, I just swam to swim. On New Year's Day 2023, I swam a mile in honour of that inspiring lady.

And with that, Anna-Rose stands up and heads out of the turnstile. A man is passing by with a small dog. She smiles, falls into step with him and starts chatting.

DANYA HARRIS

A few years ago, Danya Harris had forgotten she liked swimming. By 2023, the magic of winter dips and the friends she found at the Lido helped her complete a 5km challenge at 14.8C in the Swimathon. On a sunny May Saturday, she talks about cold, companionship and washing your brain.

I PROBABLY CAME to Jesus Green Lido when I was little, but a few years ago I'd forgotten that I really liked swimming. I hadn't swum for years, I was on holiday, and I did about 30 lengths of a little pool. I remember it was really cloudy and the pool was really blue, and I just didn't want to stop swimming.

When I got back, I got a season ticket and came to Jesus Green every single day. I think that was a year before the pandemic.

The first time I had the experience of cold water doing something magical was when I came in September before the pandemic and I was really miserable. I remember getting in the pool and it feeling really cold, and it being significant. I felt significantly better. I remember the physical sensation of the cold had a real impact on me.

Then the pool was closed for the season and I didn't swim here again until April 2021. That's when it really started to have a bigger impact. Obviously, Lockdown – I was working from home and didn't have enough interaction with people and so when the pool opened, I started coming every day and it was really, really, cold.

On the first day I came I got mild hypothermia because I had no idea about what cold water could do to you. You just don't know what you don't know.

I came back the next day and did half a length, and then one length the day after that, and the day after that, and acclimatised to the cold. I was hooked.

I don't think I missed a day until it got warmer, and the cold water wasn't there. Just as I was losing a bit of enthusiasm, I did a week's course with Colin to learn front crawl, so that gave me motivation and I started swimming every day after that. It was heading towards winter and we were wondering, is the pool going to close, and it carried on being open and it carried on being open. It was like a lifeline.

When the winter hours started, Mary, who runs the cafe, and I were a bit desperate about the pool not being open every day, and thought what are we going to do? Will Hudson swam in the river sometimes so we went down with him. I was scared up until the point I got in. And I'm still a tiny bit scared. Swimming outdoors in lakes and rivers is something I had wanted to be brave enough to do for a very long time.

The river just became something we sort of fell in love with. It was like the friendship and camaraderie of swimming at the Lido, and we were a community, and this was the first winter I hadn't hated the winter.

Jesus Green Lido introduced me to cold water swimming and whenever I am away – and I am quite militant about it – I will always find somewhere to swim outside. It's meant that when I go away I'll look up the local swimming groups like the Blue Tits and meet up with people to swim with, and it's like a really nice community to be part of, the wider swimming community.

It's something that has become really important to me. I always feel better after swimming in cold water, and that with a sense of belonging to the community here. I felt it was something missing in my life for quite a while.

When it came to the Swimathon, I swam 2.5km last year, so I wasn't quite sure I was going to finish 5km. Having people stand at the end and encourage me definitely helped. It wasn't physically harder than I thought, but quite early on the weather was very grey and everyone was finishing their distances, but then I just plodded on and got through it.

I did front crawl for all of it. I had lessons on and off with Colin – all the way through last winter and some of this winter. It is nice to have something I can work on and improve and I've constantly got something to work on, improving this little bit. It feels like it is never finished, and that is quite satisfying.

One of the things I loved about Jesus Green Lido before I became a regular swimmer was how uncommercial the environment is. Here it is glamorous, old, and unspoilt – though people would like the showers to be working a bit more – it just feels like a haven. It's a place where everyone talks to each other which you just don't get in the outside world. Even if nobody you know is here, everyone will say good morning to you.

The Lido has been here my whole life, and it's nice to have somewhere that you've been at different points in your life

DAVID REES

Since 1984, my summer has been measured by the number of swims at Jesus Green Lido. I knew that my water temperature limit was around 16C, and never thought of myself as hardy. But speaking to people in the sauna, they said, 'We just kept going throughout the winter.' No magic. No special trick.

This gave 64-year-old me a challenge. Now it's January and I'm still here. The mental health kick is better than drugs. Really I'm too thin – wrong surface area-to-volume ratio – but the poolside camaraderie is like an extra layer!

that it feels almost like a different place. Because I experience it in a completely different way than when I was little, or when I was a teenager coming here in the summer, climbing over the fence in the middle of the night. That was exciting, definitely a good memory of Jesus Green – but I'm not sure that should be put in the book.

I have mixed feelings about it getting warmer because I do like the buzz you get from cold water. With summer comes being able to swim longer obviously, and it is very hard to be sad about it because there are so many other good things about it.

A week that it snowed was really, really – I can't think of another word – special. It felt like what Christmas feels to everyone else. It snowed quite heavily. Everything was covered in snow, and it was just magical. There was ice on the pool, but mainly in the middle which was avoided.

Even when it was 1C I was still doing the front crawl and putting my head in the water which I am quite proud about!

I think the best way to sum up swimming in cold water is what a friend said, "Swimming in cold water is like washing your brain," and I really like that. You feel refreshed and not just physically, like a strange kind of ritual, like this is really important that I do it and I know I'll feel better once I have done it, and it just felt like a ridiculous thing to be doing but also so completely non-negotiable.

I'm not going to not swim.

ELAINE BROWN

Elaine Brown, 70, started winter swimming when the opening hours were extended, and kept coming.

I CAME HERE in 1959 I reckon, I used to come with my mum and dad. My mum would cook a chicken on Saturday night, and we would bring cold chicken and a salad every Sunday. I learned to swim here from the age of six. We would meet a lot of their friends, and we sat down the bottom there by the pump because that's where it was nice and sunny and warm. We were here for most of the day and my dad taught me to swim here, and I think he got a bit fed up with me because I wouldn't take my feet off the ground, so he threw me in and that's how I really learned to swim, and it didn't put me off.

I used to come in my teens as well. We sometimes used to climb over the top and in the dark – it was a sort of initiation. It must have been quite cold, and I don't remember staying in long and we used to get that sort of cusp – where it's sort of exciting or scary because someone might hear us, and we would get into trouble – but that never happened.

There used to be the hut over on the far side that sold sweets, like banana chews and fruit salad chews, which were four for a penny – they were the days.

The diving boards were in the middle of the pool. I didn't learn to dive when I was younger, it wasn't until later in my teens, and then I used to go to Parkside. When we were doing our GCSEs, we often used to come between taking our exams. We weren't meant to, but fortunately I do remember coming here once and a teacher was here, and he shouldn't have been here either, so we were caught for skiving.

I left Cambridge when I was 17, then I don't think I have been back much until the pool started to be open in the winter. I am not sure why. I think I came a few times in the summertime, but it is usually packed.

The big difference today is it's open in the wintertime, which is fantastic for us, also having the sauna. I can't even remember the showers when I was younger either. But also the cafe here. And when we have special events. The photographs, and the bring-and-share things. That's sort of made it much more of a community I would say.

Wetsuits were another new thing which I hadn't experienced, also the support because of the friends I come with. I think swimming when it was 4C was a bit like a shock to my system, but it has been supportive – willing everybody on when it was chilly and looking out for each other.

I did get hypothermia the second time I

DI BEDDOW

After the Covid pandemic I felt more than ever that daily exercise was important. As pools reopened, I tried swimming inside, but I realised I wanted to be freer and to be mindful of nature at the same time.

I joined the cold water swimmers at Jesus Green Lido and was given such a warm welcome by the community there. We were all delighted that the pool stayed open over the winter and on occasion, when I get very low, the lure of the camaraderie, the cold water and the trees against the sunrise all empower me to get up and get on. Thank you to all those who make it happen.

came. I think I'd done about three lengths and I thought, I'll just do one more, and I think it was about 4C and all of a sudden my body just went into retreat, so I was quickly taken into the first aid room and given hot drinks and my husband was rung for, because I cycle here from Histon.

My son came and picked up my bike – it was like a drama and I wasn't expecting it and it hasn't happened to me since.

It's something that has been here all my life really and I'm 70 now. It's great that it has stayed open all this time and quite a landmark for Cambridge. I know we have got the University, but I'm not really part of that. But the Lido, Jesus Green, it's just – something special you know. Not many places have their own lido and the history of it.

Since I've been swimming in the wintertime, I sort of meet friends here. It doesn't matter really as there is always someone here you know.

And everyone is so chatty in the changing rooms – and the changing rooms haven't changed much at all, and I quite like that. There is something safe when things haven't changed that much.

I'd much rather swim outside. I love looking at the sky, looking at the trees, and just how the pool looks with the sun on it. It just feels more expansive because of what you can see, and you're much more in the elements of what the day holds and I love swimming in the leaves – there is something much more natural about it and you don't get the stuffy chlorine-y smell.

I think there is something about the place, it is much more friendly when people are outside and it makes me just want to sit and enjoy the pool, whereas if I am inside I wouldn't think of sitting on the side. It means also that you spend more time. It's more sociable here, really.

There's a lot of encouragement, you know. You hear how people are or you see how they are if they are shaking. It's just that more awareness. It feels like a big family when you're here. It's like a big family.

I do like to do the crawl, but I haven't quite managed it here yet. I haven't quite got the rhythm, so I do breaststroke most of the time and I like to improve on my lengths. I'm up to six now which is pretty good for me.

I don't like to hesitate when I get in the water, I just like to go in and just do it. I just walk a little bit in and as soon as I can, get my breath caught and make a lot of sound and just go for it.

Just before I come, I do get a bit anxious – I hope I'll be alright. There's just this bit of hesitation in me, but once I get in the water it's okay. Maybe something about me getting hypothermia just sits in the back of my mind.

I always make sure before I leave home that I make a flask of drink – peppermint and liquorice tea is my favourite. That's the main sort of little ritual I gather for myself. I used to have a wetsuit and I still have it, but I don't wear it. I can't swim in a wetsuit. I feel really like a blob, whereas I do have the gloves and I do have the wet boots.

It's very reassuring seeing the lifeguards there. When I got hypothermia, they were fantastic.

ELLIE STANDEN

Ellie came to the Lido as part of her recovery from cancer therapy and besides the cold blue water buzz, found what she hopes will be everlasting friendships.

I WAS DIAGNOSED with aggressive breast cancer during the Covid restrictions, and after I finished treatment I found I was struggling. I had undergone chemotherapy, radiotherapy and surgery without my husband able to attend appointments with me, or being able to see my support network. I had returned to my job, but everything was still online. I was doing lots of running to cope with the physical and mental fallout – this worked until I injured myself and was ordered to stop running. This was September 2021, a full year after my initial diagnosis.

I was really struggling, as I missed running more than I could have thought possible. I was going to Maggie's – a great cancer charity at Addenbrooke's – to do art therapy. There I met Leanne, who was going through cancer treatment. She encouraged me to try swimming at the Lido, suggesting I might find it healing, and told me that it was staying open during the winter for the first time.

> **" As soon as I emerged from the bright blue Lido, I buzzed – all day. It felt amazing**

So this is how, on a chilly December morning, I found myself plunging in. It was a breath-taking, or rather breath-taking-away, 4.8C. I was wearing an old surfing wetsuit and I think I managed one or two lengths. Before this I had been a lover of ocean swimming, but had never swum for fitness, just on high days and holidays.

As soon as I emerged from the bright blue Lido, I buzzed – all day. It felt amazing. I met another swimmer, Danya, that day and she was so friendly and encouraging, it made the whole experience unforgettable.

My job was still online, and I think that like so many people during the pandemic, I craved human contact. I found this at the Lido. I felt welcomed, I felt safe being outdoors, and I felt happy. I met so many different people there, all of whom have smiles on their faces after a cold dip. I've also been along to adventures arranged by the Friends of the Lido, such as the trip to Felixstowe for swimming and fish and chips.

In January 2022, I realised I needed a challenge. I decided to enter the Swimathon in May that year. I trained at the Lido, bought an actual swimming wetsuit, and on the day I smashed my 5km target whilst being cheered on by my husband Craig, son Ben, and lots of friends. I'd also had lots of encouragement from Colin, the resident Swim Doctor, and had finally learned front crawl.

By meeting Danya, and Mary (who runs the cafe), I was introduced to a group of swimmers, the Goslings of Goose Green, who were terrified of not being able to swim each day when the Lido restricted its hours in November 2021. We met at 8am at Sheep's Green on the days the Lido was closed. Swimming with the same people at the same time in the same place gave me an amazing sense of shared experience, and, I hope, some everlasting friendships with the growing gaggle of Goslings.

I love Jesus Green Lido. I love the pool and the people. I love the coffee and the random chats in the sauna.

PILVI SAARIKOSKI

I ABSOLUTELY LOVE swimming outdoors and the cold, cold water, but to most people's surprise that's not why I love the Lido. It's the people here that make it special. It's rare to find spaces with community like this. I know I can go to the Lido and I'm guaranteed to talk to someone. Some days it's more important than the swim.

Left: Like many, Pilvi Saarikoski loves both the Lido's cold water and its warm community

SIMONE SCHNALL

Simone Schnall, Professor of Experimental Social Psychology at the University of Cambridge and Director of the Cambridge Body, Mind and Behaviour Laboratory, researches the ways our bodies influence our feelings. After taking the plunge at Jesus Green Lido in 2022, she hopes to use the pool as an outdoor laboratory to study the effects of cold water swimming.

I'M INTERESTED IN how the body influences how we feel, think and behave. We perceive the world through our bodies. It sounds obvious but it's also quite profound, because for a long time, psychologists and cognitive scientists were much more focused on the brain and the mind.

We now know much more about emotions, including the fact that they're based in the body. Emotions are our perception of physiological changes, like increased heart rate or the release of stress hormones.

As humans, we're so absorbed with thinking about the past or planning the future, but we spend less time thinking about our physicality.

My first winter swim was at Jesus Green Lido in October 2022. It was completely by chance. I'm not sure how I heard about it, but I ended up joining a Serotonin Swim. I'd read about cold water swimming, it sounded to me completely mad, but I was intrigued so I thought I'd just try it.

I'm not a good swimmer, I'm a head-up breaststroker. The only reason I went was because it was an organised event, I knew there would be people there who could explain how it works, and how to do it safely. I wouldn't have done it in open water. I still wouldn't. At Jesus Green you know there's a whole infrastructure taking care of you.

I'd heard people say it was 'life-affirming', and that's exactly how it felt. It really puts you in touch with your body in a way that nothing else does. It's such an intense experience, there's probably nothing else in daily life that you can do safely in an everyday environment that's as extreme as immersing your body in temperatures normally considered way too cold for comfort.

As I stepped down the ladder I thought, this is a really bad idea, this is complete madness, why am I doing this? Then I thought, I may as well just go for it, because it felt safe. Before I went in, I told one of the lifeguards to look out for me in my red fleece hat because I'd never done it before.

I was surprised by the diversity of swimmers. I expected young, athletic, hardcore swimmers. And I remember Sam Thorogood saying that the first Serotonin Swim attracted 96 people, which is amazing.

As a scientist, I was intrigued at how invigorating it was, and how wonderful I felt afterwards. There's something really interesting going on in the body, provoked by this extreme stress response. It seems like there's a sweet spot between having a stress response in the body – everything that's unfolding on a physiological, chemical or hormonal neural level – and how that feeds into a positive emotion.

I went back a couple more times, just for my own benefit because it was fun, it felt pleasant. You really feel like you've conquered a big challenge early in the morning and you've set yourself up for the day. You feel invincible.

I became more and more interested in what cold water swimming actually does to the body. What's going on?

Looking into the scientific literature, I found out there aren't many highly controlled studies. There are lots of compelling testimonies and anecdotal reports, which are provocative, enlightening and important. But the gold standard is always a randomised controlled trial (RCT). That's when you randomly assign participants to one of two conditions. It enables you to be more sure that an effect you observe isn't due to self-selection – in this case that it's a certain type of person who's attracted to cold water swimming. Without an RCT, you can't tell if your results are due to the activity or the person.

The more I looked into it, the more anecdotal reports I found about cold water swimming having an impact on mood or mental health. I also came across studies on the impact of cooling the body. They show that cooling the body is neuroprotective, which means it's good for the brain. These are mainly animal studies but it's also been shown that cooling people immediately after a cardiac arrest seems to reduce the risk of brain damage.

So it seems that cooling the body is good for the brain. It's not just about the social community swimmers have, not just about feelings, emotion and wellbeing, but something is happening in the brain on a very physiological level that's connected with cognitive function. Animal studies show that cooling increases levels of a neuroprotective protein, one that can counteract Alzheimer's-like processes in mice. I would be very interested in doing an RCT of the effect of cold water swimming on emotions and wellbeing, and also on memory.

The aims are very straightforward. Does cold water swimming improve wellbeing? And does it improve memory? We would want to have a group of volunteers randomly assigned to swimming in either cold water or in a regular heated pool. So some would swim at Jesus Green Lido and others at Parkside. They are two very different environments, so we will try to control for these additional variables, like the social community and being outdoors.

When I saw its experienced lifeguards, a cafe and first aid room – in other words a safe, controlled environment – I realised Jesus Green Lido could be the ideal outdoor lab for this research.

It would be challenging research, but if you think of the public health implications, if we find that cold water swimming has a significant impact on wellbeing and memory.

It would involve training people so that we cover all the safety aspects. We would also need to employ fully-trained research assistants who would be poolside whenever any participant is swimming so that they can collect and analyse blood samples. Analysing blood samples for the protein we're interested in is costly.

This is one of the most exciting research questions I've come across for a long time, and I've done research for 25 years. And I stumbled into it! If I'd not done it myself, I'd never have believed it. Cold water swimming should be aversive – it's a stress response – but instead it's super positive. Part of the research would be to share this evidence. All we need now is funding.

For a lay summary of therapeutic hypothermia, see www.hopkinsmedicine.org/health/treatment-tests-and-therapies/therapeutic-hypothermia-after-cardiac-arrest

EMILY SPENCE

I'VE BEEN COMING here since I was four or five, probably even before that but I don't remember. It was a lot different back then. You didn't have the lane swimming and it was all a bit more chaotic and 'nineties'.

I swim regularly in West Reservoir near Manor House in London, but I love coming here because it's so different from when I was a kid, and it's open all year round now and everyone has got into the cold water swimming. I need to check out the sauna. I haven't done that yet. And they've got hot showers here, so it beats the reservoir.

I like diving in, you can't do that at the reservoir either. It's good to get yourself immersed. I do a little somersault when I hit the water, which makes me light-headed and I forget that it's cold.

My daughter Cleo is two. She likes swimming, but in heated pools. I'll try and encourage her to swim here when she's a bit older. My dad swims here regularly, although his hairdresser told him it makes his hair green.

ALICE SMITH

THE FIRST TIME I came here I must have been five years old. Anne Garvey brought me along with her brood! Sophie Grove, her daughter, is my dearest friend. We spent entire summers of my childhood here.

There was a lifeguard called Flipper, who Sophie and I were completely in love with. We'd follow him around all day, trying to impress him.

I swam quite a lot at Jesus Green when I was pregnant. It was just after the pandemic, so I was still working from home and I'd sit up the top end with my laptop. I was apprehensive about swimming while pregnant because it can be a shock to the system. I remember my tummy seizing up, it must have been Osh inside me saying, 'It's too cold!' but it was great.

Obviously, your life changes when you have children, but I think I came to Jesus Green Lido the day before he was born. And here we are two years later and it's so nice, there are so many families here and you feel part of that. This morning we came with some friends and the children were running up and down, it's just lovely.

> **There was a lifeguard called Flipper, who Sophie and I were completely in love with. We'd follow him around all day**

ARLO BURTON, aged 6, and MAX WILDMAN, aged 11

In the first of several interviews, Annie Morgan James aka Nonna speaks to Arlo Burton and his second cousin Max Wildman.

   AMJ: What's your name?
   Arlo: Arlo
   AMJ: How old are you Arlo?
   Arlo: Six
   AMJ: Where did you swim to?
   Arlo: Over there (pointing to the first red line)
   AMJ: That's very well done Arlo! Did you find it a bit cold? That's a long way to swim!
   Arlo: I could swim further than that – probably up to there (pointing at the first steps) – but it was just a bit cold and a bit too deep.
   AMJ: You did very well for a six-year-old and you've got a nice little cosy towel on now.
   Arlo: My Nanny knitted it.
   AMJ: It's beautiful. I love all the animals.
   Arlo: Is this the longest pool in England?
   AMJ: Yes, it's the same length as Tooting Bec in London. It's 91 metres, 100 yards. They're both the longest pools. They're almost double the length of an Olympic pool. Now, is this your brother?
   Max: No, he's like my cousin.
   Arlo: No, not a cousin, a second cousin.
   AMJ: Max, can you tell me about swimming today?
   Max: It is cold, but I managed to do two lengths.
   Arlo: He's 11.
   AMJ: You did two lengths and I see you've got goggles. What stroke did you do?
   Max: Breaststroke.
   AMJ: Breaststroke, that's really fantastic. When you're 11, Arlo, you'll be able to do two lengths too. What do you both think of Jesus Green Lido?
   Max: It's very good.
   Arlo: It's cold.
   AMJ: Is it fun to be here?
   Max: Yeh!
   Arlo: Yeh!
   AMJ: Are you going to get a hot drink or something?
   Max: An ice cream!
   Arlo: An ice cream!
   AMJ: You're going to get an ice cream even though you're cold?
   Arlo: Yes! And then we're going punting on the river.

GRACE and ALICE WILSON

Papa: Alice, what do you like about going to Jesus Green?

Alice: I like going to Jesus Green in the summer, because when it's really hot you can just jump in and then you get really refreshed. And swimming is just nice. Also I love the cafe. It does really good hot chocolate. When it's really cold here I love the hot chocolate, and when it's really hot there's ice cream.

Papa: Is it easy swimming in such a long pool?

Alice: Yes, because it's long it makes you do more swimming. I like just jumping straight in. I don't know how to dive yet.

Papa: Do you meet your friends here?

Alice: Sometimes. We play in the pool, get stuff at the cafe and sit on the grass – there's lots of grass.

ELLEN WILSON

Long summer holidays learning to backflip off the diving board, hanging out with friends, desperate to get a tan, eyeing up the international students here for the summer.

Returning with my own daughters, Grace (10) and Alice (7) – left – to the reassuring familiarity of the changing rooms and poolside benches. Watching them experience the same joy.

Papa: What's the Lido like compared with an indoor pool?

Alice: An outdoor swimming pool's really refreshing and more nice. When it rains and you're swimming it's nice, but an indoor swimming pool isn't that refreshing because there's hot air and you can't get rain.

Papa: What about swimming here during the winter?

Alice: It's still really nice in winter. We were here at Christmas. It was amazing because the Mayor came, but it was very cold.

Nonna: Where did you learn to swim?

Grace: I learnt to swim at Abbey. I really like the butterfly and front crawl.

Nonna: What was it like when you first went to Jesus Green?

Grace: Actually I was pretty scared to get in because it was cold and a really big pool and deep and there were loads of people.

Nonna: What do you like about the Lido now?

From left: best friends Vivian, Frank, Francis, Gabriel and Aden

GABRIEL McGOVERN, aged 8

dear nonna i go to jesus green every week or so in the summer and in winter i dont really go because im not very confident in the water when its really cold. I like about it that everyone who wants to has a chance to always go there and try to upgrade your swimming. I userly go with granny or you or mum or aunty ellen or papa. I like to get in the water by doing a big cannon ball from the diving area and that gets me use to the cold water very quickly. After i have had a big swim in winter even though i dont go that much i like to have a hot chocolate and in summer i like to get a nice cold ice cream because the ice creams there are really good. Thats all for now bye. from Gabriel.

Grace: Oh, that's hard. I just like jumping in and stuff. I've been practising my diving and swimming, and then very good slushies. We've been with friends a few times. Some from London and some from school. There's one friend, Nancy, who comes a lot in the summer, and she likes it because she is a very strong swimmer as well.

Nonna: This is the first time you've swum in October. What was it like today?

Grace: It was definitely colder than in the summer. It was 17C. It was cold at first but I liked jumping in and then I swam a length and a bit.

Nonna: And what did you have afterwards?

Grace: An ice cream!

SOPHIE GROVE

O N SCORCHING HOT days in the late 80s, we would always arrive at the pool early and watch the space fill up until late afternoon when the water became choppy. The only sounds were splashing, laughing and the whistle of the lifeguard we called Flipper.

I remember walking to the end of the big six-foot diving board for the first time. It felt like a skyscraper. The deep end was of course in the middle and it was somewhere we treated with great reverence – the water in the deep middle was cold and dark blue, it felt as endless as an ocean. Jumping off the end of the high board was such an adventure. Later, on our birthdays Flipper would push us off the top board in pyjamas, a ritual every summer-born child looked forward to.

We lived at the pool in the summer – the concrete banks were constantly packed with frolicking, chatting, flirting bodies. We learned to swim widths in the shadowy shallow end and then breaststroke in the sunny end. We hopped about along the rough concrete paving and the space under the tall trees felt like spooky dark woods.

We grew up at the pool and only left at the very end of the day when they blew the final whistle. Back then there were no ropes and lane-swimmers would take their chances with the children, but somehow it worked. It was a kind of perfectly orchestrated joyful aquatic chaos – a place for hot kids to truly unwind and feel independent. It felt wild and free and wonderful. It was a place you met

Sophie, right, with her mum Anne Garvey

every kind of person, a little utopia. Those neat rows of towels lined up on the hot concrete kept order and the basket room housed clothes and shoes from the real world outside. I can't imagine my childhood without such a place.

As an adult I have swum as my newborns slept under the cherry tree, and taken the babies in early on in the season – they adore the fresh cool of the water. Now they are a little older and looking for safe spaces to feel free, I hope it is a place they consider their own little world. And that they can conquer the deep end and beyond!

YSMAY GILL

I have swum at Jesus Green Lido since I was a child, and this summer I am swimming here as an expectant mother.

I have always loved this Lido: as a child on the warmest summer days; as a teenager, soaking up the sun on the concrete slope; as a student, when the pool still seemed to be a towny secret; and now, whenever I can – on cool days and warm, in sun and rain, alone or with someone – as the baby grows. I am 33-weeks pregnant and the pool is the place I feel freest. I will swim here until the baby is born – then we will return together.

Baby Beatrix was born on 19 October 2023 in a birthing pool! She and Ysmay returned to Jesus Green Lido on 1 January 2024, pictured above, when Ysmay enjoyed a New Year's Day dip.

DUNCAN BLACK

SUMMER HOLIDAY SWIMS were almost always the highlight of weekends in my youth. Growing up in Cambridge was a privilege and Jesus Green swimming pool was a fantastic place to visit, since there was no seaside nearby. It was not like swimming at Byron's pool or in the murky River Cam with its clinging weeds, but it was a meeting place where kids could safely have fun in the clear water.

The pool's location by the Cam is unique. Once inside the fenced area with its grass and trees and wooden structures, there was a special atmosphere, and although it wasn't a modern lido, it had a unique feeling that I'm sure is still there today. A timeless place, rather like much of Cambridge.

In the late 1950s and early 60s, our kind parents would drive us boys and girls there early on weekend mornings. The water was chilly with the morning mist hanging over the blue pool. The first jump into the cool water was always shocking, but we soon forgot the cold and swam widths under water, dived for coins and had swimming competitions.

The best places to have fun, however, were the diving and spring boards which were not too high but stood over the deeper water in the centre of this unique 100-yard pool. In the early mornings, we pretty much had the place to ourselves and it was great to be able to enjoy that feeling of space and freedom without madding crowds. That would change for me, however.

As I grew older in my teenage years, Jesus Green was the place to meet during the summer holidays. Everyone came to cool off and socialise in the awesome surroundings. Our focus was shifting to the opposite sex and we often met on the grass beside the pool on glorious summer days. We listened to music on pirate radio stations and bought refreshments with our pocket money. We played in the crowded water and eyed the girls in their bikinis and swam between the throngs of people. Our girlfriends from earlier days were now interested in older boys and chatted together about their latest crush or fashion styles and pop idols. It was the swinging 60s after all. We even smoked the odd cigarette to look cool beside the pool, and when it was supper time we cycled home or caught the 106 bus.

Those were the days, my friend. I live in Ottawa, Canada now. And I am so pleased to hear that Jesus Green Lido is still open 55 years later!

GRACE TWINLEY and her brother TOM

Grace: We've been coming to Jesus Green Lido for the last 10 years. It used to be a big group of kids. About 20 or 25 of us. We'd walk down here, come in and we used to be here all day. Not many of us come back but I'm still here. It's a very good place and it still is today.

Tom: I like the pool; I like the deep end – which is the middle. I like diving in. It's lovely and cold and when it's hot it cools you down.

JULIE LING

I was brought up in Cambridge and over the decades Jesus Green Lido has always been a part of my Cambridge life. In the 1970s, as a teenager, my friends and I would spend afternoons at Jesus Green, jumping off the diving boards and applying Ambre Solaire to try to get a tan. Trips home from London in the 1980s always included a dip at Jesus Green. Since the 1990s I have lived in Dublin, where I swim regularly in the Irish Sea.

I always visit Jesus Green on trips home. My nephew was a lifeguard at one time, and taking him and my son to swim on Boxing Day 2022 was a particular highlight, especially the post-swim flask of hot chocolate and brandy.

NAOMI WORTH

I come to Jesus Green Lido because my granddad – Francis Jeans – lives here, and he comes here every day so he takes us and we go for some swims.

I really like it because you can go in for a swim and it's really refreshing and then afterwards you can get a hot chocolate. My granddad is a good swimmer, I guess, as he does it all year round.

Naomi with her granddad, Francis Jeans

Fiona, Rowan and Robin all enjoy a swim at Jesus Green Lido

ROBIN and FIONA TODD

Three generations of swimmers are interviewed here: Robin Todd, her daughter Fiona Todd and Fiona's son Rowan Oliver, aged 2

AMJ: Have you been swimming, Rowan?
Rowan: Yeh!
AMJ: What was the water like?
Rowan: Cold!
Robin: We brought our children here in the 1990s, mainly in the summer. Now, the Lido's open year round and it's fantastic. I come down with my daughter sometimes, like today, and she can swim while I take care of Rowan.

I come at least a couple of times a week and in the winter, maybe once a week for a shorter swim, but it's wonderful. The thing I really like about the Lido is it's all inclusive. When you walk through the door it doesn't matter who you are, where you're from or what you do – everybody's friendly. It's a fantastic community. And I hope that in Rowan's lifetime he'll be here many times too.

Fiona: I have been coming to Jesus Green from when I was about two, the same age as Rowan is now.

I think of the pool in many different ways – in childhood it makes me think of summer and coming to just hang out here. The first time I got stung by a bee was here. We used to hang out and jump in and out. It's always been cold and so it's been quite fun. As an adult, I've done cold water swimming and come here all year. I swam here when I was pregnant; it's just lovely and amazing exercise.

And Rowan has just had his first dip at Jesus Green today.

ELLEN NOWAK and family

Seven memories from seven family members, thanks to Ellen (formerly Ellen Bailey).

Liz: It was the summer of 1976, which was a really hot summer. It was my O-level year, so I didn't have to go into school much and I was waitressing at the colleges. We used to wait tables at breakfast at the college, go into town and get a coffee, go and serve lunch, go to Jesus Green and spend the whole afternoon down there, and then go back and serve dinner. Every day. I remember that the diving boards were in the middle of the pool, because that's where the deep bit is. We all just used to lie around in our bikinis chatting up the boys.

Linda: It was 1958 or 1959 and I was at St Andrew's junior school in Union Lane (now St Albans). They used to take us weekly to Jesus Green for swimming lessons. It was absolutely fantastic, and we used to have so much fun. We used to talk about who was fun in the pool and who wasn't. It was so, so cold, but as a child the cold didn't matter to me at all. I also used to swim in the river in November! When I was a teenager, Jesus Green was somewhere you could go and just lie out on the banks and sunbathe. There was no sun cream whatsoever, and what we would take was a pot of Nivea or olive oil – we thought it was the thing to do to get a suntan.

Will: When I was about 15 in 2001, we used to congregate on Jesus Green in big groups of 30-40 kids. We'd sit in a big circle on the grass and drink the cheapest booze known to man and smoke joints. Every now and then someone would get the idea that we'd break into Jesus Green after hours, so we'd climb over the fence and skinny dip. The first pair of boobs I ever saw was at Jesus Green!

Daniel: Went there once to dip my toe in. Too cold. Never went back.

Peter: A friend of my wife's was a well-known flâneur and he decided he wanted to be a model. At the time, I had a twin-lens reflex box camera, and he asked me if I would take moody black-and-white photos of him lounging in Jesus Green. I've still got the negatives somewhere.

Ellen: There was a summer in the early 90s when me and my school friends went to Jesus Green every single day, no matter the weather. It was such a great place for teenagers, in that bit before you're old enough to go to the pub. Happy days!

Maria: I'm a swimming teacher and took my boyfriend there to teach him to swim. It didn't go well for either of us. He hates any sports that I'm better than him at.

NATTY BARNETT

I've been going to Jesus Green for six years – every time I stay with Grandma (Ruth Barnett). It's mostly cold but that doesn't matter. I never get in down the steps, I just jump in.

Everyone is happy there and everyone is very friendly. I love the picnics we have with Grandma and Vicky (Bursa). I also love the kiosk, especially their hot chocolate. I'm glad it's near where Grandma lives. It's great that it's such a long pool so it would be a good place to learn to swim (like Grandma did).

If you want to go swimming in Cambridge, go to Jesus Green. Why go to an indoor pool?

CAROLE ELLISON and her granddaughter RUBY REED

Carole: I've been coming to Jesus Green Lido since about 1980, when my children were small, four and six years old.

We used to hang out here all the time in the summer. Then, I used to come all the time because the children loved it; it was very sociable and you could talk to people whenever you liked. It was just a great place to be.

Later, my daughters Camilla and Lucy and then my grandchildren came here. I think that's quite typical of people who come here, different generations of swimmers following in their family's footsteps.

Ruby: I've been coming here for as long as I remember. I came together with my mum and my grandmother and it's always

been such a happy, family-orientated place. It's a haven in the city and a bit of an escape, a great place to relax and just cool down.

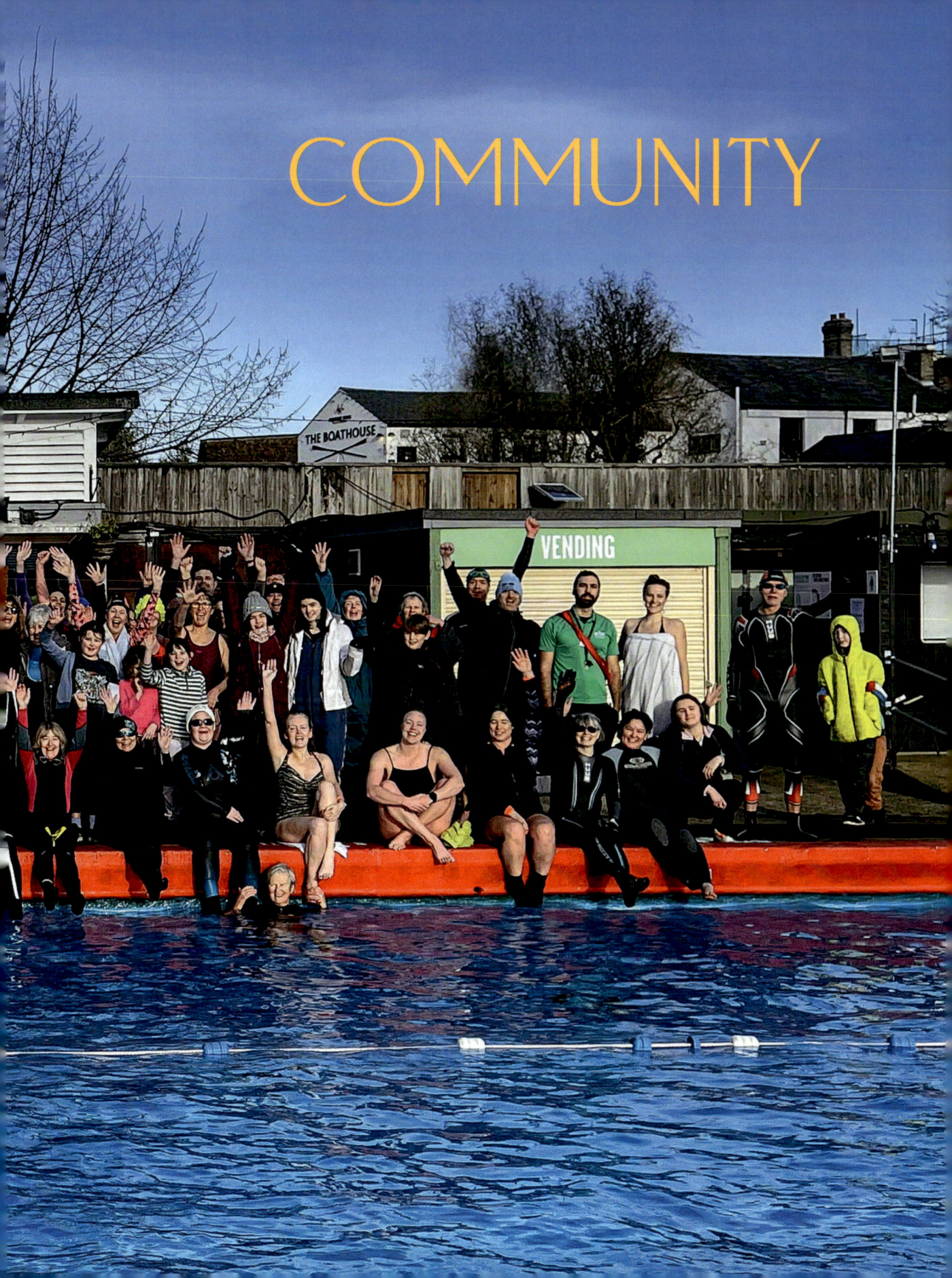
COMMUNITY

DUNCAN GIBSON

WHEN I LIVED in Dunedin, New Zealand, I thought I had to go surfing for peace of mind. In Cambridge I started swimming at the Frank Lee Centre to keep fit for surfing. One night I was told I couldn't swim but could join in water polo. This morphed into Channel swimming, and during cold water training at Jesus Green, my love affair with the Lido commenced.

Then the epiphany: It wasn't surfing that is the elixir, but the fresh dip. A saviour after a day's teaching around Cambridgeshire.

Warding off sleep, just needing to get to the pool to wash the day away. A nap on the grass.

A new man.

Sometimes, on crowded sunny days, a wide circle of sunbathers around me as I awoke to the realisation of a snorer. Somehow, I had become part of that eccentric seasonal devout set of cronies – the ones I would meet in public and say in a loud voice that I didn't recognise them with their clothes on. Now back in New Zealand, this time in Christchurch, it's these cronies I miss at my gas-heated 33m summer pool.

EMMA BATEMAN

I'VE BEEN SWIMMING at Jesus Green Lido since 1984. I started my nurse training at Addenbrooke's Hospital in 1982 and didn't discover the pool for two years – I was thrilled when I happened upon it one day cycling along the river.

The pool is absolutely my favourite place in Cambridge. I have so many happy memories. Before I had my son, I swam every day whatever the weather. When I was on maternity leave, I pushed the buggy to the pool and swam my lengths whilst lovely smiley Mary and co. watched Noah. He started going in the pool from five months old and he never complained about the cold. It makes me proud that he continues to swim wherever he goes.

I have met so many people at the pool over the years. It has such a wonderful atmosphere.

Here's to the next 100 years.

MELISSA SANTIAGO-VAL

SINCE I WAS a teenager, the Lido has been part of the fabric of my life in Cambridge. What I especially love about it is that Jesus Green is more than just a swimming pool. You see all life there, all people in our community – from the regular swimmers, triathletes, old friends, teenagers, former colleagues and teachers you never thought would be swimmers – and you get to see a different side to people.

Over the years, I've made some great friends at the Lido, going to a 40th birthday in a college garden through a friend I met there, and another friend who sadly has now passed away. We had our last wonderful conversation about life walking around the perimeter of the pool. Some people I only see in the summer when I swim there, and I love to wonder what becomes of everyone when the gates close. Of

Right: 'The Big Shiver' with Arthur Rank Hospice, May 2019

course now the pool is open all year round for the braver souls, some people don't have to wonder anymore!

It's a place that brings so many aspects of Cambridge life together and diminishes many 'Town and Gown' elements of our city.

The crispness of the cold water has turned many sluggish days into productive ones, although I'll admit that I prefer to keep my bikini swims to when the temperature is above 15C as I really don't enjoy wearing a wetsuit.

I'm so proud that our city boasts such a unique, and incredibly long, lido mimicking the path of the River Cam.

We are so incredibly lucky that the Friends of Jesus Green Lido and Better keep the pool alive, help to remember the history and preserve its uniqueness for generations to come. Before body-positivity was a thing, it is something Jesus Green has always nurtured: it allowed us all to feel comfortable in ourselves and accept others. We could all learn a lot from that.

COMMUNITY

Pregnant Suzanna and, inset, Iona and dad Simon

PENNY WILSON

ChatGPT said: "Open-air unheated swimming pool located in Cambridge, offering a refreshing escape and a vibrant community hub for swimmers and sun-seekers alike." But so much more. Through the turnstile is a different world: where everyone is a companion whether alone or in groups; where home is a bench, identity is a towel or robe, a suit and a cap and a greeting as much as a name; where order is the watchfulness of the lifeguards and knowing one's lane; and the high life is the cafe. Water, wood and grass, an oasis of sanity through the seasons. Perfection.

SUZANNA WATSON

I HAVE BEEN coming to the Lido since we first moved to Cambridge in 2019. To me, the Lido has always felt like a place where every person is welcome. I love that no matter who you are, where you are from or what is going on in your life, this is a place where you are welcome.

It helps that I'm a person who finds immersion in cold water incredibly therapeutic, but Jesus Green Lido is about more than just the joy of swimming. The community of regulars that I get to see gives me a connection to know that all is well in the world. I am a clinical psychologist and work with people who have experienced horrible trauma, and I have personally always found the Lido a sanctuary before or after work, particularly during Covid when I was so grateful that the Lido was open.

For my own personal story, I have loved being able to swim at the Lido throughout my pregnancies. After nine miscarriages, there was lots of anxiety about my first pregnancy and whether or not I 'should' be swimming in cold water. However, just as the emerging literature is telling us, every swim was a physical and mental tonic, no matter the temperature and no matter the weather.

The kind faces at the Lido didn't know our story but delighted in my growing belly and when Iona was born, they were equally kind. I swam the day before my

C-section and was back in the water (for a very, very slow length) two weeks afterwards.

Iona was 'swimming' in the Lido as soon as she could be (with a little neoprene to help). If I get her wetsuit out at home, she only associates it with big smiles and the kindness of the people we get to see at the Lido. Thank you Jesus Green Lido for all you have done for me and my family.

SINÉAD RYAN

On a hot September day, Sinéad Ryan shares an emotional return to Jesus Green Lido following the birth of her son Oisín – an absence of 12 months.

IT'S THE FIRST time I've come here for a year. I used to swim here every summer when I moved back to Cambridge from London four years ago. And I'd come every morning before work.

I had my baby boy Oisín a year ago, so this is my first swim at Jesus Green Lido since I had my baby! And it feels like me! It's lovely! You just feel all refreshed and alive. And part of a community that's always been swimming here. It's so nice.

I was thinking just now – maybe I'll get a wetsuit and come back in the winter now he's a bit older. Before, I couldn't get that freedom as it's a half-hour drive for me. Maybe now.

I swim four times a week indoors but it just doesn't make me feel the way the Lido does … I don't know why I'm getting so emotional. It's just different. I love it here. And I'm going to come back next week with my friend, and she's going to babysit while I have a swim. It's lovely here.

CATHERINE HAYHURST

WHAT does Jesus Green Lido mean to me? I have swum here on and off for years. An occasional short fit of triathlon training enthusiasm, some sunny days and a great option during Covid.

I remember remarking once how nice it would be to swim and then sit in the sun with a book and cup of tea, but instead we always headed off.

This year I'm recovering from long Covid, with short swims followed by a book and a cup of tea! Since meeting lots of slightly mad winter swimmers, I've ditched the book – my fingers are too cold and it's more fun to chat.

SUE GORDON-ROE

A Jesus Green regular for half her life, summer swimmer Sue Gordon-Roe loves the Lido's mix of sociability and solitude. On a late summer day in August, with wood pigeons calling and signs of autumn, she talks about friendships, belonging and the therapeutic environment the Lido provides.

I'VE JUST REACHED the great age of 70, and I've been swimming here for 35 years. I can't remember how I discovered it; I really wish I'd got going on it earlier, but life was such that I didn't.

Right: Street artist Giacomo Bufarini, known as RUN

I learned to swim in Newmarket outdoor pool, and as a child I swam at Parkside pool. I was 10 when Parkside opened and it was the most exciting place in the world, to be able to come on the bus from the outskirts of Cambridge – we lived in Queen Edith's Way – into the middle of town with my friend and go swimming on our own. Newmarket pool was cold and it wasn't pleasant, so at the age of 10 a warm pool was the best thing ever.

I brought my daughter Alex here when she was nine or 10 and she loved it. For a few years we had her birthday party here – in the grassy corner by the pump room. There'd be a dozen of us, Alex's friends plus two or three adults. We'd sit in this corner with a great big picnic, and it was a great place to have a July, end-of-term birthday.

The children loved it. They could run around and scream a lot. I remember one little boy who came in brand-new trainers, and when his mother came to collect him he only had one. Nobody ever found the second trainer again. It might have been on a roof or in the river, and I felt so bad handing this child over with one brand-new trainer.

But Alex liked Parkside, she'd swim there with friends, so I've mainly swum at Jesus Green Lido on my own. Hugh, my husband, sees it as my place. What I love about it is the mixture of sociability and solitude: being able to be sociable and being able to be on your own. When I was still working, being able to come here and hide behind a book – a sign that I was busy – was essential.

Working in mental health was often quite stressful and this was complete relaxation, very quickly. It was a haven, an oasis after a full-on, busy day. After work, it gave me a gap, it wound me down. I still feel that now, because of the time of day I swim.

Now I love the social bit – which I describe as the village green. There are two or three levels of social here. I rarely plan to meet anybody but I nearly always do. And I have a word with whoever's here. Today I had a word with a woman I haven't seen for six months. Brief, but very nice. There are times when little groups form; I've enjoyed meeting them and knowing they'd be here. There are

> **Swimming outside is so different from an indoor pool – being able to look at the trees, the clouds, the seasons**

people who I only see here, who I don't meet outside the pool, so the pool feels like coming to another country.

I'm a summer swimmer – and that probably won't change. There's one man who, when I see him in May, wishes me a happy new year and I know exactly what he means. We've all arrived in this new country, and we're going to be here for four or five months, and it's very nice.

But I'm aware now that there's a whole group of all-year swimmers. I love that for the pool. My interaction with this is that if it's a nice winter's day and the sun's out, I come in. The lifeguards don't mind,

and I carry on the 'village greenness' of the place.

I usually come late afternoon or early evening. That suits me well because it perks me up for the evening. I'll sit and chat for a bit, and then swim. As most people know, I have a little routine in the water: I walk up and down, and then do some exercises to strengthen my arms by trying to get out of the pool without using the steps. It's a bit like an annual MOT. A couple of years ago I struggled to do it so I've had to fix that.

I often don't stay in the water long. I only do four lengths. I get very cold. I have got a wetsuit although I've only worn it four times. And I shower here, I love the 'outsideness' of that. Some years we'd stay in the communal showers for ages just nattering. After my shower I like to do all the pampering, the body cream. My skin's probably at its best when I'm coming here.

In the winter I swim at Parkside or Abbey, but not as often as Jesus Green, and I love swimming in the sea. I try to keep swimming once a week but increasingly I'm enjoying walking in the winter instead.

Swimming outside is so different from an indoor pool – being able to look at the trees, the clouds, the seasons – the little winged lime fruit that spiral down in summer and the leaves in autumn. It just feels freer. I'm not sure I have the words to describe what makes it so wonderful. Time of day alters what it looks like too, whereas Parkside always seems the same – it's always brightly lit and stinks of chlorine. Here, I don't smell of chlorine afterwards. It's a real joy.

I'm swimming against the tide, but I'd like Jesus Green Lido to be heated and for us to go back to season tickets. I understand the change, but for poorer children in Cambridge, being able to buy a half-price season ticket once schools broke up and have six weeks of being able to come here every day was like being on holiday for families who couldn't afford to go away.

The cold water is reviving – and not only from work stresses. During the last two summers of my mother's life, Jesus Green Lido was a very 'holding' place because there were certain people I could talk to. We shared a lot about elderly parents and the loss. The pool was very special then. And I think for other people at different stages of family life, from stressful teenagers to bereavement, this can be a place that's partly out of time, in terms of ordinary everyday lives.

Friendships here can be very therapeutic. A therapist is somebody who isn't a particularly close friend, but a safe person in a safe place. That's why people often describe the pool as a haven and an oasis. I don't think anyone expects therapy from others here, but perhaps we inadvertently give it.

I wonder if that's because many of us come on our own rather than with a partner. Obviously one or two people

come with their significant other, and families swim here – you sometimes see three generations of families swimming and that's lovely too. But that's more common in the outside world.

You feel like the place belongs to you. That's how I felt with my season ticket. I bought it and it was mine! You feel you have a place here, you belong. It took me a while to adjust to the fact that the Lido's open in the winter, but now I just come and sit here. It might be February and I won't come to swim, but I'll come to sit because it's my place.

JANE FIRMAN

Addicted to Jesus Green Lido sparkling
  blue water:
Plunging its depths scattering diamonds
in ice, snow, sun or showers
is the freshest most exhilarating wake-up
  call …
To be alive in that moment!
Be welcomed. Be together. Be alone.
Have space, intentions, goals.
Do nothing more than arrive – not even
  swim.
Still – You are part of a community of
  swimmers.
Maybe one of the early group with
wetsuits, goggles, time and distance on
  their minds. You
swim one length, maybe two, aim for
  four, swim twenty-two.
Swim 100 lengths of the 100 yard,
  100-year-old pool.
Bliss.

LAURA TURVILL

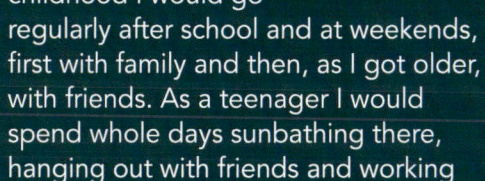

JESUS Green has always been a precious part of a Cambridge summer. From childhood I would go regularly after school and at weekends, first with family and then, as I got older, with friends. As a teenager I would spend whole days sunbathing there, hanging out with friends and working on my tan. Now I love the start of the season when the water is cool and fresh and there are fewer people.

It's lovely to sit on the warm wooden benches with your face in the sun to warm up after a swim. The simplicity of the changing sheds adds to the charm. Regulars are relaxed and friendly and there's usually someone to have a chat with.

Jesus Green Lido is really one of the best things about Cambridge.

IN MEMORIAM
NINA HALLOWELL, 1957 – 2023
BY GINNY MORROW

I FIRST MET Nina Hallowell nearly 30 years ago, at the Centre for Family Research in Cambridge, after she had taken up a researcher's role having recently been awarded a DPhil from Oxford. Nina was a kind, loyal and thoughtful colleague and a generous source of support. We hit it off straight away, quickly becoming good friends.

Our friendship evolved to Jesus Green Lido, and we became firm swimming buddies. We spent many hours at the wonderful Lido in all weathers. Nina and I loved it there, basking in the sun, chatting, swimming in the cold, drinking tea, and we shared fits of laughter when struggling out of swimming gloves and tops.

We also enjoyed family holidays in Cornwall together when my children were small, and celebrated Christmases, weddings and the arrival of my grandchildren.

Professionally, Nina was an academic nomad. From Cambridge she worked for the universities of Edinburgh and Newcastle, and would seek out various opportunities for a dip while visiting academic colleagues in Australia or the Fondation Brocher in Geneva, where she delighted in swimming in the majestic Lac Léman.

Nina and I were in touch to the end, swapping books, texts, and the last package she sent was a bottle of anti-chlorine shampoo, with a message saying she didn't want my hair to go green. She left me her Bondi Icebergs swimming hat, a couple of beautiful necklaces, and a card that read, "Just keep swimming for me, and when the pool is particularly clear and crisp think of me."

Thank you, Nina, for wonderful memories of a life well lived and those magical times together at Jesus Green Lido.

Poet and cafe operator Maurizio serving up mulled wine for Lido swimmers on Boxing Day 2023

I love the Lido at Jesus Green
Early morning, blue serene
91 meters down by the river
By tall lime trees that gently quiver
In early summer it's like a fridge
Still nowhere better in Cambridge
It soon warms up as summer goes by
And yellow leaves drop from the sky
Established, like a worn cricket bat
91 years with dark timber slats
It's paradise, come bake in the sun
Then swim this cool pool, it's so much fun!

Maurizio Cavaliere, 2014

FRIENDSHIP

CHARLIE ROBERTS

RUNNING IS MY first love but the Lido has made me question my loyalties. In the decade that I've lived within stumbling distance of Jesus Green, I have always felt an urgency to get in the water if it's open. Awaiting so keenly the first day of the season, dreading the last day of the season. Thank goodness for the winter opening hours these past few winters.

But why? What quality does it have that running can't quite match? Obviously the feel of the water on skin, but also on 5mm of rubber wetsuit, boots, gloves and two hats? Yup. The water supports me and holds me up. The Lido took the weight of my unborn child for me that first summer, swimming when pregnant with a gigantic baby boy, the water gave me buoyancy. The Lido is where, later on, I finally learnt to master front crawl. A new trick!

The Lido knows many of my joys. The Lido has also heard so many of my troubles. The water hears my bubbly breaths and washes the worries away – for a bit, at least. I always smile when I get out. But it's not not just the water. The humans of the Lido are magnificent. The lifeguards who freely gave me top tips on my front crawl and shared my joy when I completed my first length without that drowning feeling; we have the best lifeguards. The wonderful women who chat in the summer hours and my new winter swimmy buddies all enhance my life in ways that can't really be explained. Shared endeavour? It's somehow more than that at the Lido.

My kids have grown up with the Lido too. We would bring picnics after school when they were little, and both of them gained their water confidence here when their limits were only up to the red lines. Now they happily bash out lengths – just as we're about to leave, obviously – and they dive like penguins and lead balloons in the middle section.

One Easter holiday they both came and helped repaint the woodwork – they are part of it too. Even my husband gets in when it's warm enough. And they all know to make sure I get a birthday swim, or a weekend swim, or a morning swim, or even a post-run swim, because I do still love running.

JANE WOODIN

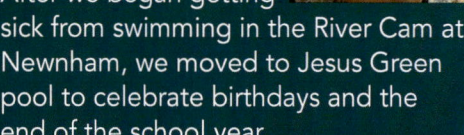

When I was a teenager in the 70s, I would meet friends here. After we began getting sick from swimming in the River Cam at Newnham, we moved to Jesus Green pool to celebrate birthdays and the end of the school year.

I don't ever remember it being called a lido then, but what's not changed one bit – and what struck me when I returned here aged 58 – was the smell of the wooden changing rooms, which takes me back to those years of schoolgirl celebrations every time I come.

It is often autumn when I manage the trip back here: colourful leaves in the water, a long fresh and peaceful swim, timeless and full of voices of the past.

Jane's paintings were inspired by her love of swimming, with Jesus Green a major focus

JANE KEATE

I TURNED 50 the summer before the centenary. I have been swimming here since childhood. I remember my dog-eared junior season ticket made from card, costing about £14 in 1980.

I have continued swimming throughout my life – swimming between shifts at the Royal Mail sorting office – until today when I swim in the afternoons to recover and restore after my daily postround delivery.

I have made such good friends at the pool. I've been wild swimming in the UK with Caroline Scott. Judith Stone and I took part in the cold water swimming championships at Tooting Bec Lido in London in the winter of 2011. Becky Allen helped me plan a trip to Berlin where I swam in Schlactensee and the River Havel.

These are the highlights of my life. My wellness, my fitness, my friendships and adventures all started at Jesus Green Pool and the pool is where I always return to swim and share stories.

> **Jesus Green gave me the confidence to enjoy water, to thrive not just survive in water, and that's a life skill which is so important for young kids**

MARTIN LOWN and his daughter KATY McLARNON

Swimming lessons at the Lido didn't teach Martin Lown to swim, and he was never as fast as classmate Christine Jarvis. But the Lido did give him the confidence to become a swimming teacher himself.

MARTIN

It must have been around 1957 or 58, when we would leave Arbury Primary School and walk in a snaky arrangement along Carlton Way, down Stretten Avenue, and make our way to the pool. I was about eight or nine.

I was a contemporary of Christine Jarvis who was in my primary class and became an Olympian. She competed at the summer Olympic Games in 1972 and 1976. She certainly was a better swimmer than I was. I think I was probably a faster runner than her.

When we arrived at the pool it would be, "How cold is it today?" It wasn't that welcoming – you just felt there was this body of water and you had to get in – but you know, we got in at 56F (13.3C) and we somehow had to learn to swim in those freezing conditions. As it happens, I don't think I learned to swim with the lessons. I do remember the lessons. Holding onto the ledge, kicking your legs behind you – the traditional things. Then launching out with a float and counting how many kicks it would take you to make it to the other side and then grabbing the edge at the last minute.

But it was when I came on my own and was throwing myself around down the end there, thrashing around in the water, I realised I was swimming and holding myself up. So clearly, coming as a child from primary school gave me that confidence and I came back wanting to swim more and more.

There are always high jinks in changing rooms with kids. I have clear memories of the "cattle sheds" as they were called – the long open changing rooms, not single cubicles – where we changed, and the diving boards. I loved that springboard, with that bit of matting at the end and you'd sort of spring up and down and then finally plop. In those days it was setting yourself goals – jumping in, then jumping from the first board, then the second board and so on – you were allowed to jump and you were allowed to dive.

I remember getting the 14-yard certificate. That was clearly a goal to get across the pool. We also had swimming

Left: 'The Big Shiver', May 2019

galas here – races across the pool and probably races as far as the 50-yard point.

I did hang out here as a teenager and especially after GCEs. The slabs down the end were a sun trap, and I would just hang around there, chill out and run and dive in. That was the best thing about coming, being able to run and dive in; I loved it. It gave me the confidence to enjoy water, to thrive not just survive in water, and that's a life skill which is so important for young kids.

So, I ended up teaching swimming to primary school kids. I am passionate about learning to swim as young as possible because I had that privilege and the confidence from those early days and it stays with you, you are not fearful of water.

Mary and I encouraged our own children to get into water and they learned to swim very early. I recall my second-oldest granddaughter playing here for hours when she was about 13 or 14. They'd be in and out the water and they would stay forever, just as I would do as a boy.

The brick pump room hasn't changed. All the surrounding stonework is the same, but now we have the lovely clearance of the trees which has made such a difference. It is open and beautiful, and you can see the sky when you are swimming up and down. That's really very special.

Being here outside makes all the difference. It's a very special experience. People are ready to chat, they are open so there is the sociability side of it, which is very strong. Then there is swimming under the blue or grey sky, whatever it is, and being outdoors and the sparkles and the light you get and there isn't the smell of chlorine. It's just the natural light, the

sky and the lovely turquoise colour of the water.

I get in quickly, I don't muck about prepping. I like to do four, five, six, seven, or eight lengths, and then get out and get warm and just lie in the sun.

Mary, who runs the cafe, is a great character. She is so passionate about the place. The lifeguards are really good. I've got to know Gabriele a bit and one tries not to distract them too much from their job when it's busy, but I think they seem to have a sense of serving the local community by being here.

The corner where the pump room is is the best place to sit in the evening when the sun goes round. It's a bit like Henman Hill at Wimbledon where people gather. I think the grass has grown better since the Leylandii trees came down.

Sitting at the end of the pool in the sunshine as the sun goes down, with the

warmth and the glow of that final end-of-day swim – what a lovely thing to do before going home. It's a wonderful place of relaxation and tranquillity, mentally, emotionally, physically. A place of wellbeing.

It's great place where you feel the whole rhythm of life. Meeting old friends, making new friends and acquaintances, sitting talking to people around the poolside. Meeting parents of former pupils which is always rather lovely, catching up with their kids. Meeting people you haven't seen for a year, if it was just a summer swimmer returning.

I'm delighted to come and chat to whoever is here. As you talk to them you just feel a sense of belonging. I am not that successful at reading here, there are too many people to talk to, or close your eyes in the sun and just fly, but if I can read a book then I do. It is a bit of a hidden secret, down by the river, behind the trees.

KATY

I'VE GOT A vague memory of being at the grassy end of the pool with my mum and another family when I was very small. And then memories of being a teenager and being at the paved end with friends. When I came back to Cambridge my children were little. We used to come to the pool, and I would pack up picnics and they would play in the pool for ages, my youngest would sometimes stay in for like three hours at a time.

I also have memories of the really long queue and being hot and it taking forever to get in. More recently, it is somewhere I often bump into people who I haven't seen for a long time, sometimes people I was at school with. But whoever you meet, it's always relaxing.

Lido regulars, from left, Lindsey, Danya, Annie, Sylvia and Charlie

RUTH BARNETT and VICKY BURSA

Two friends talk about how they got into lunching at the Lido.

Ruth: It's our hobby!

Vicky had served me tea at a garden party and then we met again at Jesus Green, having discovered our lifelong love of swimming and food.

Our Lido self-catering began with one or both of us suggesting we bring a snack to the Lido to eat after our swim. This followed many discussions about recipes, childhood meal memories, foraging and cooking tips. We seem never to stop talking about food. Whenever we decide to bring a picnic to the Lido we don't plan in advance who is bringing what. We don't shop specially. Often it's 'what the house gives' – a direct translation from Czech, Vicky's first language. Miraculously every time it turns out OK. We never fail to be absolutely delighted. In fact, we are always delighted with our delight. "Wonderful!," says Vicky. "Yum!," say I. "What a treat. Aren't we lucky?!" both of us say.

If the weather is inclement, we sit in the shed or the snug. We're very flexible! Our picnics bring us great joy. Such a simple thing, sharing food.

Vicky Bursa and her daughter Margaret Bursa, who for her 40th birthday had only one desire – crab sarnies with her mum and a JG swim. Ruth is pictured on page 177

> ❝ We enjoyed our coffee and cake after our swim and this made it possible to stay a little longer, swim more or chat

Lunch at Jesus Green contributes to the sublime experience of swimming, socialising and laughing.

Vicky: When planning to swim at Jesus Green Lido with my friend Ruth, we would quite often say, "I'll bring a coffee," and "I'll bring a cake." We enjoyed our coffee and cake after our swim and this made it possible to stay a little longer, swim more or chat.

As the days got warmer we decided to extend this to a lunchtime picnic. That way we could stay into the afternoon and not have to leave in search of food.

We seldom planned what we'd bring, it was a case of what we found in the fridge and cupboard. But every now and again, to make it special we brought an embroidered tablecloth and laid one of the picnic tables, using napkins and small plastic plates with cutlery. Sometimes other swimming friends joined us and brought their delicacies to share. We were delighted to share food with other swimmers. Everyone was most welcome.

I always remembered to send a photo to my children, so that when my daughter was going to have her 40th birthday, she chose to spend it at the Lido and have a picnic after. She wanted crab meat sandwiches. And she got them!

We look forward to more in the autumn – and when it gets too cold, at one of the other pools.

FRANCIS JEANS

On an August morning at the pool, with the sound of water and wood pigeons, artist and retired school teacher Francis Jeans reflects on the cast of characters – from 'Brown' David and 'Gizmo' Geoff to 'First-class' Richard and 'Happy' Mary – who have peopled the pool over the past five decades.

I'VE BEEN SWIMMING here since 1975. That's 48 years. Can you believe it? At first I came on my own, in that very hot summer. Since then, I've been a regular season-ticket holder and never missed a season until the first Covid Lockdown. I brought my children here from when they were very young, and they both learned to swim here.

The pool's not changed much over those 48 years. It's retained its character. The old changing sheds are still as they were. The difference is the addition of the showers and toilets at either end. But the character has remained the same. Where the sauna is now we had a cafe, a black hut that opened both onto the pool and onto Jesus Green itself. It sold teas and coffees, lollies and ice creams for the kids plus the odd sandwich or sausage roll.

Over the years, I've learned that each of us has their own issues and problems, but finds coming to the pool a godsend: a place to clear the mind and wash away the troubles of the day. The times I've heard this expressed in different ways over the years is beyond count. It's the same for me and when I walk through the turnstile I sense that I'm entering another world.

Entering this world of course involves meeting friends doing the same. Meet-ups with other regular swimming friends and the chance of a chat or a laugh is all part of the Jesus Green experience. It cannot be found anywhere else. Indoor pools don't offer the same space and ambience for such essential social interaction.

My routine is always the same. I swim first and then sit, always in the same place, on the right at the men's side, and enjoy the pool or chat. And coffee is essential after a swim; if it's not available here I head for the Kiosk on Jesus Green or Kerb Kollective at the Cambridge Museum of Technology. I probably drink too much coffee.

I swim in the river as well as at Jesus Green Lido. For me, the pool is probably the best thing about living in Cambridge. Honestly, that's no exaggeration. Swimming here is very important for social reasons, for mental health, physical health.

Swimming outside is particularly important in the winter when there's lack of light. There's a challenge to be met with outdoor swimming, and usually that's to do with cold water. It's hard to explain, but I always feel better afterwards. It needn't be a very long swim – in fact during the winter the most I can tolerate is two lengths. You just feel better for coming through the turnstiles, that moment of rounding the corner and seeing a few like-minded nutters.

I suffer from depression, and there have been times – like one summer when there was a lot of stress through work at school – when I've been very low and couldn't swim. Instead, I'd come to watch other people swim, because just being here

and knowing that others were enjoying it, even if I couldn't, perhaps helped lift me. There's something about the continuity of it.

The pool has also been somewhere I paint. Over the years my work has changed and developed. I went through a phase of wanting to paint people in a new situation, and I thought the pool might offer it. The problem is that it's a moving target, but I never want to rely on photographs, I've always got to go back to the real subject.

Although Jesus Green's a moving subject, I tried to make it more graspable by focusing on reflections looking into the basket room. People would pose for me – lifeguards on quiet days when the weather was poor, and there was plenty of that – or swimmers who'd pose for me on the steps for 10 or 15 minutes.

Of all the people I've met at Jesus Green during five decades, Terry Gorham stands out. He was a great character, extremely sociable, witty, amusing, and a great mimic. He had a habit of giving swimmers nicknames. It was his way of remembering people. He would talk about 'Health and Safety Will', 'Brown David', 'First class Richard' and 'Gizmo Geoff'. There was 'Happy Mary' and 'Pile of ironing Sue' because she'd always say "I shouldn't be here wasting time. I've got a pile of ironing at home that needs doing." Although Terry has died, people still remember all these names.

For many years I met Terry regularly at the pool. He travelled a lot for work, and he'd often ring me from his car and say, "I'm five miles from Cambridge – see you at the pool at 6 o'clock." We would both have had stressful days but we'd have a

> ❝ Swimming here is important for social reasons, for physical and mental health. It's the best thing about living in Cambridge

laugh and a chat and the stress would be forgotten for a while.

Terry was full of anecdotes about characters he'd seen that day and characters at the pool, although there was one swimmer he was always keen to avoid. When he saw them coming he'd say "Got to go!" and dash up through the men's changing sheds and out through the turnstile.

But we always made time for swimming, and we managed to swim off our frustrations. Sometimes we'd have a good moan, if something awful had happened. But we'd somehow always end up with a laugh. Many laughs actually. He was an absolute joy. And at the same time, we could talk about our problems and put the world to rights, particularly over politics.

When I first started swimming here, Terry was also a new kid on the block and he'd sit with old Ron who was holding court. Ron would swim one length, very slowly, and then sit all afternoon at the sunny end and talk – pausing only long enough to draw breath – about his life in the Army, particularly in India. Ron was a short-back-and-sides chap, you could tell he'd been in the Army. But he loved the place. I guess he was very lonely. Terry gave him a lot of time, he was aware that he needed somebody; that's how good Terry was as a young man.

Terry's daughter Claire was a great swimmer. She's a bit older than my daughter Lizzie but they got on well and as youngsters spent hours at the pool together. That gelled our friendship. Terry and I were very different, yet we remained great friends over many years. The day of Terry's cremation a group of us decided to go for a swim together at Sheep's Green, and held a minute's silence.

LISA TURVILL

Jesus Green Lido has always been a huge part of my life for as long as I can remember. When it was normal as a child to take a picnic and stay all day with my friends. As I got older, swimming before a shift at Browns and hanging my bikini on the fire exit bars (much to the manager's annoyance). It was – and still is – the best thing about living in Cambridge.

Gus Siddle was another great character, and one Terry also focused on. Gus strode up and down the side of the pool, arms behind his back and chest pushed out, wearing the tightest pair of trunks. When Gus wasn't looking, Terry did a great physical impersonation of him, he had such a gift for mimicry.

Terry would sometimes say, "What is it about people here? Everybody is gifted in some way. They can sing or dance or paint. And then there's me, I can't do anything." So I wrote a whole sheet of foolscap listing all his gifts – his humour, his wit, his social skills – and gave it to him, but he wouldn't really look at it. He was polite about it but he always felt inferior in some way.

Over the years, we've been blessed with some great lifeguards here. Not every year – one year they had to bring in the Army to help staff the pool because staffing was so difficult. Ed Durrant stands out as a particularly good lifeguard. He's still in Cambridge, working at the Leys School. He's well-built and had real gravitas – he could deal with any kind of trouble.

Ed's sister Julie lifeguarded here too and works for Cambridge City Council. Terry used to call them the Durrant Dynasty. Julie he called Mother Superior. Their other sister's called Joy. Talk about aptly named, she gave so much of her time to this place. She worked at the YMCA and borrowed their minibus to take a group of Jesus Green swimmers for a day out at Brockwell and Tooting Bec lidos.

Over the years we've had excursions by train to other pools, in London and beyond: Parliament Hill, London Fields, Charlton, Letchworth, Peterborough,

Hitchin. It's a form of solidarity, a form of outreach from Jesus Green. We always introduce ourselves as coming from the Lido in Cambridge and we are always given a warm welcome.

Each year, the Friends of Jesus Green hold a winter party in January. In the beginning we'd hold them in people's houses and the first – at Simon Crowhurst and Alex Buxton's – was fancy dress. I went as the pool, dressed in swimming trunks and cap with lots of bubble wrap and rubber ducks. Kieran Toon – a regular and a very good swimmer who moved to

people talked about depression at that point.

As a result, one year I even decided to enter the world of Ceilidh dancing in a town and gown group, which I continued for a few years as a way of alleviating depression. For a while it was good, and one of the people I met dancing was Vicky Bursa, a regular swimmer.

Around the millennium, we came up with the idea of a day at the seaside in October as a way of relieving the depression. At first we went to Dunwich to swim and have fish and chips at the wonderful Flora Cafe. But the beach shelves very steeply there so we decided to move the sea swim to Felixstowe, preceded by a coffee at the Fludyers Hotel and followed, of course, by fish and chips.

Before I started swimming in the river, the thought of a long winter without outdoor swimming was awful. We were all forced into indoor pools where there's no sense of meeting friends, congregating, sociability, they're just not built for that.

Probably the best thing to have come out of the Covid pandemic has been this resurgence of interest in outdoor swimming. The pool decided to experiment with winter opening hours and it was a great success. Long may it continue.

Swimming outside is essential for health, fitness, mental health during lockdown and after – that's been proved by the popularity of the pool in winter. I never thought I'd swim at 4C with a rash vest, but I do. It might only be two lengths but I feel so invigorated by it, and there's the sociability. If you've not tried it, I'd really recommend giving it a go.

Birmingham – dressed as Jesus but all in green.

Every September, at the end of the season, we'd hold a party on the afternoon of the closing day. People brought food to share, and we'd sit along the bench at the ladies' end where the sun stays longest. By mid-September the water would be cooling, and the afternoon was always tinged with sadness because we knew that the following day we wouldn't have the pool anymore. We all wondered what we'd do without it, and lots of

CARLOS TORANZOS

Carlos has been swimming in the Lido since 1975. In the heatwave of 1976, he remembers some kids helping him sneak his daughter's pram over the fence for an after-hours dip.

I ARRIVED IN Cambridge December 74. I am a political refugee from Chile. I was 22 and had just finished my studies in Chile, and I wanted to continue studying and so Cambridge was a good option.

We discovered there was a pool, and they wouldn't open it until May, so we swam in the river. When the pool opened in May, it was a very big difference. We had to pay to get in and it was a bit grotty. They had these baskets you collected when you walked in and then you would segregate boys and girls and women and men.

We would go to the right for men and left for the women with our baskets. The water was freezing, it was always very cold, and the weather wasn't terribly pleasant in 1975, and so we would bear the cold because when you came out the sun was shining, and it was lovely, lovely and very many people would come with their families. It would become a focal point for families.

Someone died from swimming in the river and contracting Weil's disease, so we could no longer swim in the river. Jesus Green Pool became the place.

My first daughter was born in Cambridge in December 1975, and we would go with her to the pool, just a tiny little baby. The water was far too cold for her. I then had two more daughters. Jesus Green was a must.

In this fantastic hot year 1976, that was the year when the pool really, really became an absolute necessity to the people in Cambridge. It was incredible, I mean it was the only place and the sad thing is that they would not really keep the place open. You know they were very rigid with the times, and you were told to get lost. It was far too hot. They would close about 6.30pm or thereabouts.

But people were very cheeky, and they would go in the evening, and they would climb over the fence, and everybody knew, and we would sneak in. I remember going with my daughter and

> **In this fantastic hot year 1976, that was the year when the pool really, really became an absolute necessity**

being helped by those kids to pass the pram to the other side – it was incredible, incredible. We were young and… I don't know. The majority of people who went in the evenings were young people.

It was the centre of activities, particularly in that hot summer of 1976 and then after that in 1977, 1978, it was very much a focal point for meeting. You would go there in the afternoon after lunch and you would meet people there and it was always, always full. If we were meeting people with kids, we would choose to go to Jesus Green. The problem was that the water was very, very, cold indeed and the kids would not

stay in longer than a few minutes and you had to be in the water with them.

In those days, there wasn't any kind of clear division for swimmers, the whole pool was just open so sometimes you would be swimming because you wanted to do a length or two and then suddenly you'd be hit by someone, or you would hit someone. If the pool was full, it was very hard to swim. So, it wasn't really a come and swim place, it was come and get wet and enjoy it and be together!

The essence of it was that it was a social centre for people to gather, you knew people as well because their kids came and started playing together and then the parents would arrange a next meeting there and then you'd have your picnic as well. We were about 300 refugees from Chile, and I would have thought we had about 30 to 40 youngsters from the age of 20 down, and the teenagers would go more on their own and they would gather there.

I remember, to enter the pool you had the turnstile and a little girl got stuck there. It was incredible, we had to wait for the police and the firefighters to come. It took at least half an hour, and she was getting very agitated, and we were trying to comfort her and the parents. All trying you know; we used every single technique and the experts suddenly appeared from nowhere and they knew exactly what to do. Nothing worked until they cut the thing. I think that day they reduced the gaps between the bars, you see.

Cambridge summers were associated with the pool. We didn't have any money to go anywhere. I mean Spain was far too far away and even going to the beach, we didn't have a car and the bus service was very irregular. If you have the pool here, the pool becomes your centre, for people of low income particularly. It was the only place we could go and enjoy, really. It was our summer space.

The pool was nice because you could guarantee it was clean water. With the river you never knew, and you were always a bit suspicious, it was very muddy and difficult not to swallow a drop of that water.

The children – as teenagers they would meet with their mates and go to the pool and then they repeated the tradition of the parents, and they would climb over the fence and sneak in, because the pool operators didn't change the times until very recently. We had to tell the children off and not to go, because it could be dangerous. They would say, "Oh God dad, you're old fashioned!"

PAUL MORGAN

Paul Morgan learned to swim at the Lido – sort of.

I WOULD HAVE been somewhere around 12. I went with my school, the Manor School group. We had to change in the changing cubicles, which were wooden with a bench inside and a wooden door on the outside. It was all boys, as the Manor School in those days was split into a girls' half and a boys' half and we never met at all.

It was all very new to me, being so young. I had not really been swimming at all. I probably couldn't even swim either when I first went there. You might call me a late learner as far as swimming is concerned. I certainly wasn't swimming as a small child.

We went first lesson in the morning. So, we had to be at the swimming pool by 9.00am and the masters would be there already waiting for you.

It was May time, and the water was very cold. I was a little runt of a boy, I didn't have much flesh on me in those days. I just remember it being freezing cold and putting my arms around myself to keep myself warm and just a pair of speedos or whatever I'd be wearing.

They had a pole with a hoop to help people learn to swim. I would go down the steps at one of the shallow ends and obviously you weren't expected to swim a length.

When they were teaching you to swim it would be across the width. You could just about touch the bottom.

The height I was, I could probably just touch the bottom with my head just above the water. I would have bobbed across with my feet still on the bottom making the movements with my arms. I learned the basics of swimming and by the time I went on holiday to Ilfracombe that first year, I was able to swim.

As a teenager it was a summer thing to congregate at the pool, if the sun was shining. It would be easy to get there on a bicycle and I would go with my friends either who were at school with me or were neighbours.

My older brother Barry (who's passed away now) went there a lot. He and his friends at the time were all apprentice engineers at Cambridge Scientific Instruments which was right opposite the pool on the other side of Chesterton Road, where the Job Centre is now.

I remember a cafe where we bought snacks and things. And the diving boards, but I would not have gone near them

Meg, second from left, and Eleanor, furthest right, enjoy a splash at Jesus Green with friends for the Lido's 70th birthday

as they'd have frightened me to death. So there was a high one and two lower ones, they were right in the middle at the deepest part.

Jesus Green Lido is a great asset to the city and it always has been.

MEG PLATT (née BATTERSBY) and ELEANOR GODFREY

Meg: I've got such fond memories of Jesus Green Lido. I loved going on the first day of the season in May; it didn't matter what the weather was like, we'd be there and swim for hours. It was the start of my love of cold water swimming. I don't remember going with my family, just hanging out at the pool with lovely friends and having so much fun. I think we scratched our initials onto the changing room doors and then always used the same one with our initials each time we went back.

Eleanor: I have very fond memories of spending hours at Jesus Green after school. Come rain, wind or shine, we'd be scouring the bottom of the pool for coins. One day I found a fiver. I remember being best mates with the lifeguards and playing on those giant floating mats. Those were the days.

Acclimatising

CHALLENGE

DIRK GEWERT

After becoming a regular swimmer in his 50s, Dirk Gewert unwittingly embarked on a swimming journey that changed his life. From Jesus Green Lido to the 20 Bridges Swim around Manhattan via the English Channel, swimming for him has morphed from exercise to therapy – a way of silencing an inner voice telling him he wasn't good enough.

I STARTED SWIMMING regularly in my 50s. At first it was for exercise, in an indoor 25m pool. Gradually, swimming became more of a therapy; it was 'me' time. On a good day I could let my thoughts drift into a zone where lengths just went by without any apparent conscious involvement from me. I sometimes thought that I'd fallen asleep while swimming.

I live just a few minutes walk from Jesus Green Lido and so one summer's day I gave it a try. Oh, bliss: less turning round, sun on my back, ample lane space. OK, sometimes the water got a bit cold, but the changing conditions from week to week just added to the swimming 'thing'. Little did I know then that I had embarked on a swimming journey that would quite literally change my life.

I don't know where the first spark of the idea to take part in an outdoor swimming event came from, but one day around 2010 I found myself standing at the start of the annual Bournemouth pier-to-pier swim. When I finished the 2km swim I cried: me, at the age of 55, swimming 2km in open water! What a great feeling. I wanted more.

If I could swim 2km, why not further? The river Dart 10k: tick! The Thames Marathon (14km): tick! Lake Coniston (8km): tick! The Hellespont in Turkey: tick! Lake Windermere (18km): tick!

Where is this taking me? Most of my regular swimming was still in Jesus Green Lido, and I had started swimming in the sea at Felixstowe and Dover. The English Channel was staring me in the face. Really? Wasn't I too old to swim 36km, too slow, too unfit? But I have come to realise that one of the reasons I undertake challenging swims is precisely to overcome those inner voices, those demons, that have all my life been telling me, 'You can't do this, it's too difficult, you're not good enough.'

And so it was that in 2019, after months of intense training in the Lido and at Dover, and four weeks short of my 64th birthday, I swam from England to France in a little under 16 hours. The oldest person to do it that year. And in October 2023, a few weeks after my 68th birthday, I swam all the way round Manhattan Island in New York (48km) in just over 10 hours, with some help from the tides.

What next? Who knows, maybe just some lengths of Jesus Green Lido on warm and sunny summer days. But if I do undertake another big challenge, it will simply be because I want to, and because I believe that I can.

> **The changing conditions from week to week just added to the swimming 'thing'**

EVIE ANEMA

In July 2023, just two years after her first summer swim at Jesus Green Lido, vet student Evie Anema took part in the biennial Oxford v Cambridge Channel relay. Less than a month later, she successfully completed a solo Channel crossing. At the Lido, she says she finds a place to switch off from the pressures of student life.

I'M A STUDENT at Newnham College, in my fifth year of Veterinary Medicine. There's only one more year to go so it's very busy, which is probably why I love swimming so much. It's a break from everything else – time to relax and do something different.

I've been a club swimmer since I was 11, and started open water swimming competitively when I was 16. Those were mainly wetsuit events but two years ago I had the chance to be part of the University of Cambridge Channel relay and thought I'd give it a go.

At our first training session at Jesus Green Lido the water was 12C. I couldn't imagine getting in without a wetsuit at any temperature, let alone 12C, but I did. After 15 minutes I was freezing, it was horrible, but I came back because I loved it afterwards. I've swum outside for the past two winters. When it's coldest it's head-up swimming but once it's above 10C I'll put my face back in the water.

The first winter was really interesting. Some days it's colder but you can swim for longer; it's very dependent on mental determination each day. And you meet more interesting people during winter because people who do it are crazy, that's the only way to describe it, but also really interesting.

There's a better sense of community at the Lido than an indoor pool, and it's not the kind of place where you get people pushing in front of you. Everyone is really friendly, they cheer each other on, so you always leave feeling like you've achieved something. There's definitely a different mindset at the Lido compared with an indoor pool – and that's something I really enjoy.

I'm part of Cambridge University Swimming and Water Polo Club, which also includes an open water swimming team. There are two major events – an annual swim at the Henley Classic and a Channel relay swim every other year.

Cambridge doesn't have a great track record against Oxford in the Channel. In 2021 we lost by 45 minutes, which in Channel swimming terms isn't a huge margin (it took us just under 10 hours). We'd only had eight weeks' training due to Covid, and given most of us hadn't done any cold water swimming, we did well.

In 2021, our Channel relay started swimming from Dover at midnight, rotating swimmers every hour. I did two legs, so my first swim was in the dark, which I'd never done before, but my biggest problem was getting really seasick on the boat. Swimming is usually a very individual sport, and I'm not a huge fan of team sports, but it was lovely to be part of a team. We'd all gone through tough times together and it was lovely to cheer each other on. Eventually making it to France was really exciting.

Our time in 2023 was 11 minutes faster – 9 hours 47 minutes. Oxford couldn't swim on the same day as they couldn't get

an observer for their boat. They finished in an amazing time of 9 hours and 3 minutes. It was such a shame to not be able to go together so we can't say how much the conditions affected both of our swims, but I'm super proud of the team!

My solo was a huge challenge: I felt seasick for the whole swim and there were many times I wanted to get out, but with the help of my amazing support team I was able to land in France in a time of 11 hours 14 minutes. When we set off it was 1am – dark and raining. I've only swum in the dark during my two Channel relays, each for an hour. During the solo, I swam for three hours in complete darkness – it was terrifying and demoralising and I've never been more grateful to see daybreak.

I used the solo to raise money for Pathways Care Farm in Lowestoft. It is a farm, but it's also a place that provides a caring, healthy and therapeutic environment. My grandpa had dementia and went there for respite. Since he died five years ago my grandma's been a volunteer there, and I wanted to help other families get the help ours got there.

The Lido plays a big part in our acclimatising to cold water. The first session at the Lido was the first time most of us had done any cold water swimming. Jesus Green's a safe place to give it a try. Today, I've come on my own, whereas I'd never swim in the river by myself. With lifeguards and other swimmers around, the Lido feels really safe, and that gives everyone an opportunity to try cold water swimming.

Veterinary medicine is a full-on course

Left: Evie Anema finishes her solo Channel swim

with lectures all day, every day on most days, plus practicals. You have to see some difficult things. So it's important to have time away from that, something you choose to do. Swimming lets me switch off. For a while, other things don't exist except the sound of the water.

One of the best things about Jesus Green Lido is its length. You rarely bump into people or catch anyone up. Because it's so long, you don't feel like you're competing. Indoors, when you're next to someone it can feel like a race. Here it feels really different and I love that.

My first swim here was in summer 2019, my first year at Cambridge. It was 17C so I thought I'd wear a wetsuit but because nobody else was in one, I thought, "I can't put mine on!" I did about four lengths and was so cold when I got out. I thought, "This is horrible – why would anyone do this?" In early 2021 I came back, did four lengths in 12C, got out, got back in, and never looked back. After struggling so much with the cold, it's amazing how you can build up that cold tolerance. If you're determined, you can do so much more than you ever thought possible. It's amazing.

I think cold water swimming changed my life. When you get out of the water, you feel like you've achieved something, which can be hard to do otherwise, especially somewhere like Cambridge which is full of high achievers. When I go into the Vet School everyone always asks if I've done a cold swim; they're always excited. Even when I've finished training for the Channel swims I'll keep swimming at Jesus Green – it's somewhere you always come away from feeling better than when you arrived.

SOPHIE ETHERIDGE

When county swimmer, lifeguard and triathlete Sophie Etheridge suffered a life-changing cycling accident in 2011, she wondered if she'd ever return to open water swimming. In 2023, she set a world record for the longest English Channel solo swim. She talks about accessibility, training at Jesus Green Lido, and how she's working to raise awareness of disabled swimming.

ACCESSIBILITY IN OPEN water swimming is vital and necessary. After an accident in 2011 I was left with multiple health conditions – I needed to use a wheelchair, I stopped all sports, I felt like I could no longer participate. But when I was ready to return to open water, I found nothing but kindness and compassion from the swimming community, including the lovely Jesus Green Lido.

A couple of years after returning to swim events, I realised that there weren't any other people with disabilities, at least none who I knew of or could see, taking part and I didn't know why. So I decided to create the Adaptive and Disabled Open Water Swimmers (ADOWS) group. It's a place where those with disabilities can ask for advice and support and where coaches and event organisers are able to ask how they can be more inclusive and accessible.

Since creating the group, things have changed drastically for me. After a few big swims and my coaching, writing and advocacy work, a series of happy coincidences meant that in November 2022 I suddenly found myself signed up to swim the English Channel in August 2023 – solo!

I trained hard through the winter, both outdoors to stay acclimatised and in my local pool too, all the time learning as much as possible about taking on the English Channel.

I did many of my longer swims in lidos, including Jesus Green, where I could do long, cold swims in safety thanks to the lifeguards. And I had a few key weeks and weekends during my training where I travelled to the coast and focused solely on sea swimming.

August came round much too quickly; I was in Dover waiting for the call to meet my boat and when it came, I felt a mixture of disbelief about what I was about to attempt and also the utter insanity of the situation.

I had planned for a maximum of 20 hours of swimming but currents, tides, jellyfish and Complex Regional Pain Syndrome had other ideas. Every stroke was a fight, but after 29 hours 4 minutes I finally crawled up the beach in France and landed. Not only had I achieved my dream of swimming the English Channel, I set the world record for the longest ever English Channel solo swim.

I wanted to raise awareness of what those with disabilities can do, show what we're capable of with the correct support, and remind people never to put a limit on their abilities because with the right mindset you can go further than you ever thought possible.

For more information on the Adaptive and Disabled Open Water Swimmers group visit their Facebook page: www.facebook.com/groups/adows

Kate Downes on her leg of the Channel relay in 2022

KATE DOWNES

WHEN A TEAM of ladies from Norfolk decided to embark on a Channel relay, I jumped at the chance to join them. We booked our swim, third slot on the neap tide starting on 20 June 2022, with an experienced Channel swim pilot, Stuart, and his boat the Sea Leopard. We decided to name our team 'Channelling the madness'. Over summer 2021 we had been swimming together at Sea Palling and Lyntord Lake, sharing our excitement and fears for the swim.

In autumn 2021 it started to get real. We needed to do a qualifying swim, two hours in water below 15C. I decided to do mine at the Lido.

It was an overcast Wednesday afternoon when I left work early and arrived to find Jesus Green at 13C and Gab (Gabriele Scarmatto) and Val (Moore) on duty. I told them of my plan and Val agreed to keep an eye on me. As I swam up and down the pool, with a few hot chocolate stops, Val counted my strokes to check I was OK and offered words of support.

While my serious swim training moved indoors, swimming regularly in the Lido over the winter kept me acclimatised to the cold, and meant that by mid-April I could do longer training swims outside. Training in the sea started in May, but as I could only get there at weekends, the Lido became my training ground.

I can report that the Channel relay swim ended up being a lovely day out with the team. We started as the sun rose over Dover on 23 June 2022 and finished at Cap Gris-Nez about 14 hours later. The sea was blue, calm and warm, the support we had from everyone was amazing and we raised lots of funds for the mental health charity Mind.

I LOVE JESUS GREEN LIDO
BY KATE DOWNES

I love the submerged golden leaves in the autumn that make me feel like I am flying.
I love the cold of the concrete floor on a hot summer morning.
I love the pattern of the sunlight hitting the bottom of the pool.
I love the challenge of a long swim when it feels like the pool is working with me.
I love the joy of choosing the changing room with a coat hook.
I love the feeling of raindrops hitting my swim cap.
I love the sunrises and sunsets and the red light reflecting off the pool.
I love the feeling of safety that the lifeguard team provide.
I love the blue fairy lights and how they signal the colder months ahead.
I love the sounds of the Lido on a busy summer's day.
I love the blue of the sky and the clouds that change positions with every breath.
I love the chop of the water when the triathletes are training.
I love the red painted wall and how it signals my progress.
I love the misty mornings when the end of the pool almost disappears from view.
I love the clouds of steam that come off the outdoor showers in the cold air.
I love the feeling of belonging to the Lido.

SARAH COX

IT WAS A hot summer afternoon. I had planned to meet my dear friend Di Brown at the Lido for a refreshing dip. As is tradition on a sunny afternoon, there was a slight queue on entry. While waiting, we noticed a laminated sign that was slightly tucked away from view.

This plastic coated A4 sheet contained a challenge. More precisely, a challenge involving a rubber duck. A duck rescue challenge, no less.

The aim of the mission seemed simple: to transport a rubber duck from one end of the Lido to the other, hands-free. On the poster there were age categories. From reading it, it was unclear if adults were allowed to enter. Well, this sparked a discussion between us, and with time on our hands standing in the queue, the goading began.

At no point during this conversation did we discuss technique (this will become relevant later in my plight). When it was

our turn at the booth, the fresh-faced slightly perplexed lifeguard confirmed, after figuring out which poster we were referring to, that we could indeed take part. He would just have to get his colleague to invigilate our attempts at the said duck rescue.

We went through, saw the glistening water and made our way to get changed in the familiar musky, dark wooden cubicles. We discussed who was going first and decided that it would be me. I regret this decision in retrospect.

So, there I am, facing the long strip of azure blue water, sun above my head, eye to eye with my duck, which I later discover is called Conington. I am ready and I am eager. The bemused lifeguard is leaning over me with his stopwatch.

The challenge commences. We are off!

My first thoughts are: swim using breaststroke, with Conington in between my arms, nudging him with my head. I learn early on that this will not work. Conington drifts off from side to side, I have little to no control, the Lido is very busy, and the duck is very wilful.

I then try kicking Conington. I have little success with this. I can feel the lifeguard cringe and look embarrassed, and although I cannot be certain, there may also have been eye rolling. I, however, will not give up: a challenge is a challenge after all. Conington with his yellow plastic head and cartoon eyes will not defeat me!

At one point I even try to bite Conington's head. This does not work either. I keep thinking it must be possible, or there would not have been a poster. Eventually, exhausted and depleted, we arrive at the other end of the 91m pool.

I am sure Conington had a smirk on his little ducky face. The concerned lifeguard tells us our time – 4 minutes 30 seconds.

Now, it is Di's turn. Goggles on and perched ready to swim, she pops her duck in between her legs and swims with ease to the far side, gliding in at an impressive 1 minute 55 seconds.

I finally understand my mistake – being a literal-minded person, I thought you could not touch the duck with your hands at all.

Our names are then written on the leaderboard. Luckily, no one else has taken part. I claim a well-deserved second place.

Till we meet again, Conington!

DAVID LYNCH

I discovered this hidden gem 15 years ago when I was training for Buddhist ordination. It became a safe green space to withdraw to when life's demands started to overwhelm. It offered a visceral, sensual release from the heady pursuit of wisdom and truth. I started making friends with other 'retreatants' who seemed to welcome the invitation to talk about the joyful release of cold water. It starts with a short sharp shock as I ease myself in, then the mesmerising blue as my head submerges, followed by a building sense of release as muscles and mind open to the power of water. Jesus Green Lido is my sanctuary.

LINDSAY JAMES:
JESUS GREEN, BY A 90s TEEN

A special place, a retreat of its own,
Special to summer in Cambridge alone.
No mist on the commons, no winter fair.
No more freezing chill in the air.
Summer has come, the sun's high and bright,
And beams on my face as I get on my bike.
I ride past the Fort, stand on top of the bridge,
As I take in the view of the rowers beneath.
The postcards and Cam – only Cambridge can know,
Cows stand and stare, as folk come and go,
And chew on the grass,
It's free Commons, you know.
I get to my target,
There's a queue to get in.
Turquoise water shimmers in light,
A mirage of utter delight.
I set up my towel, I warm in the sun,
Try to suck up my courage, to get there and run.
I get to the steps, dip my toe, then I know
I won't get in that way, it's a no-no-no-no!
So I bomb in the middle, body aching with chills,
My breath taken away, as I'm filled full of thrills,
Now I'm ready to go, my arms bursting with joy,
I'm floating along like a humanoid buoy.
I swim in the water, great shimmering light,
I swim and I swim, filled with delight.
I try to do eight, as that's half a mile,
In sections of two, as I'm here for a while.
I meet lots of people with stories to tell,
Many ages with lives, many cultures as well.
My friends come and go; I'm not leaving this place
And I spend the whole day with a book in my face.
I eat my packed lunch my mum's made me with love,
And get an ice cream to cool in the sun.
The day goes so quickly, near time to run.
I jump in the water, the cool comes from above.
I swim in tranquility,
Smiles all round me,
All unique in some way,
All enjoying their day.
As you leave Jesus Green, a part stays in your core,
A sparkle of love, a shimmer of light,
As it's always a place that promises more,
A joy and a pleasure, a treasured delight.

GREG ALVEY

I WAS BROUGHT up in South London, and much to my great fortune there was a lido at the bottom of my road – Bellingham Open Air Baths. I was taught to swim there by my mum, a woman with no aversion to cold water.

From a young age an annual season ticket was purchased for me, 25 shillings I think (£1.25 in decimal money or roughly £27 in today's money), and I grew up, into my teens in the 1960s, using the pool as a second home. I met my friends there, listened to music on early battery-operated record players, dived and bombed off the boards.

Eventually I moved to Cambridge, but trained as a lifeguard and went back to London for a couple of summers and worked long hours on the poolside. Tragically, after a couple of cold summers, the mindless decision was made to close the Bellingham pool in 1980 and build some flats.

What fortune I had to have moved to live in Cambridge, with a beautiful lido just down the road.

Since the mid 1970s I have been a regular at Jesus Green. What great joy there was to be had when, after a long day at school, I started to do my lengths, mentally abandoning all the stresses and anxieties of the day. Front crawl, always front crawl. No disturbances or distractions. No bell ringing, no questions to answer. Breathe to the right, one, two, three breathe, one, two, three … Count the number of strokes in a length – 127. Half an hour later, a quick shower then home. Endorphins aroused. Calm descended.

Greg's Lido-inspired art

My children were introduced to the joys of picnics on the poolside, learning to dive in the 'deep middle'.

One of the great joys is finding a quiet spot on the poolside; somewhere to read, listen to the cricket, snooze. It is also lovely to have a quick chat with the regulars – people from all walks of life.

I found this poem the other day which I wrote in Addenbrooke's Hospital in August 2021 following a major operation. I could see the weather outside was glorious, and I longed to be in my second favourite place in Cambridge, Jesus Green Lido:

Call me Cool Swim
In this crystal pool all cares leach
Heaven begins.

JO-ANNE FOWLES

Jo-Anne Fowles is a nurse consultant in intensive care at Royal Papworth Hospital. She reflects on a swimming childhood in Western Australia, feeling happiest in water, and what Jesus Green Lido was like when it reopened during the first Covid summer.

I'M FROM WESTERN Australia, from a tiny country town called Kojonup. The road signs there said 'population 2,500' and even in a town that size we had a 50m Olympic-sized pool.

I've always loved swimming. My mum used to say that I was happiest in water, more coordinated in water than on dry land. When my twins were teenagers, if I was in a bad mood they'd tell me to go and have a swim.

Some of my earliest memories are of swim training. We'd be training in the morning and the evening. I think I've always been happiest in water. It's a combination of the silence and the rhythm, you can just meditate.

Up until the age of 12 I was a competitive swimmer. I was the Western Australia state butterfly champion so I'm a skilled swimmer. Now I swim freestyle and backstroke. I wouldn't say I'm fast anymore but once upon a time I was.

I did my nurse training in Fremantle, Western Australia and came to Cambridge in 1987 to work in paediatric intensive care at Addenbrooke's Hospital. After a couple of years I moved across to cardiothoracics at what was then Papworth, now Royal Papworth Hospital.

But I didn't discover Jesus Green Lido until the 2000s when my children were involved in WaterAid concerts. Since then I've swum 4km – about 44 lengths – three times a week. Every year on my birthday, I swim a length for each year I've been on the planet. I don't have any speed or any aim, I just go up and down in my own little world.

When I get into the pool my brain's full and when I get out it's empty. It's important processing time and I problem-solve while I'm swimming. I know exactly how long it takes me to do my 4km, it never changes, so I don't need to count lengths but I do. The rhythm of counting keeps your brain out of the dark places.

When you swim indoors it's exercise. When you go to Jesus Green it's meditation – all your senses are caressed – it's that sort of place. When I go through the turnstile I expect utter, utter peace and that's what I get. It's like an oasis.

As an Australian – and I'm very, very Australian – nothing in the UK can be better than Australia. But for me, this is the best water I've ever swum in. It's a combination of the length and the fact that it's rarely busy enough that you have to be aware of other people in the water. Turning onto your back, doing backstroke and seeing the sky and the clouds and the trees.

It only took a short length of time for people to know who I was. Someone always says, "How are you, how's work, how many lengths are you doing today?" It's like a village. It's a really respectful place. No-one ever stops me when I'm swimming. No-one taps me on the head to say hello between lengths – they know I might not be amused if they did that.

This morning, it was just such a lovely misty, sunny morning; that sort

SIMON TIMBERLAKE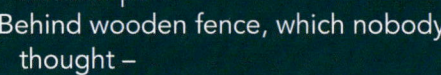

Lido Blue

Next tethered bikes
  on river front
By turnstile click and
  window port
Behind wooden fence, which nobody
  thought –
Gather stalwart swimmers on wintry
  days
And noisy crowds in summer haze
A place for nymphs in bathing caps,
in wetsuits, goggles, bathing wraps
They come for sun and frigid water
Disciples of Cambridge sanitoria.
This non-spa town pool of light and
  colour
For total immersion there is no other
place to swim a hundred yards, for a
  hundred years
And self renew
No North Sea grey or Cam Green
Just Lido blue

of connection between the mist rising and the sun coming out. There's a bit of an autumnal feeling now. Getting undressed in the fresh air and feeling the sun's warmth on you, I love that. And the outdoor showers.

Jesus Green Lido has a vibe that's hard to describe unless you've experienced it. And the lifeguards take on the spirit of the place. They're not over zealous but you know you're safe. If you watch them do the little swim tests for kids, they always do it in such a lovely spirit. It's almost like the vibe of the place and nature softens everyone's edges. I think my retirement job might be lifeguarding at Jesus Green.

During Covid, one of the things I missed most was swimming. I remember going back to Jesus Green Lido for the first time in 2020. Even now I feel really emotional thinking about it. Because we'd been on the front line. I specialise in ECMO (ExtraCorporeal Membrane Oxygenation) which is for patients who have such bad lung disease that conventional medicine can't support them. Covid is a good example. The sickest Covid patients came to Royal Papworth as one of the five ECMO centres in the UK.

It's been an incredible experience, and really showed the best of people. But seeing the volume of very, very sick, very, very young people, and working the hours we were, and doing what was expected of us, with the personal protective equipment, the threat to our families and ourselves from the virus.

Because I work in a high-stress environment, swimming has always been a coping mechanism, so to not have it … I have some photos of me trying to swim on the garden table but it didn't have the same effect!

Jesus Green reopened around 25 July in 2020. Going in on that first day and just sitting on the edge and putting my goggles on – I had to take them off because I was crying so much. It felt like I was back in my happy place. It was the most glorious, glorious thing. The water was only about 16C but sliding into that chilled water and just being able to stretch to the other end, I could almost feel myself being put back together again.

SYLVIA FERDIN

I'VE BEEN SWIMMING all my life. I come from Italy and started swimming when I was four because as a very little child I didn't have much appetite and my parents thought that sending me swimming would help. And it worked. It made me hungry and now I love food.

I've lived in Cambridge for about 20 years and swum at Jesus Green Lido all that time. It's a charming place. I love the scenery, the nature, the wildness of it. You always meet interesting people. And of course the swimming pool is beautiful.

I have a love-hate relationship with the leaves in the autumn. Sometimes they really annoy me but on a day like today they look so lovely. I'll have to take another picture.

Today I swam 12 lengths because the temperature is going down. In the summer I swim up to 10km.

I'm a masters swimmer and swim competitively. My last race was in Sheffield last weekend at the Swim England Masters National Championships. It was an exciting weekend, full of swimmers breaking World, European and British records non-stop every day.

I broke the British record in the 1500m freestyle for my age category – 55-59 years – which is probably my best event at the moment. My time was 19.44.85, I broke the record by 14 seconds but I can do better. I can always do better!

I also swam the 400m individual medley, which I like, the 200m fly and then the 400m freestyle to finish the weekend.

LAWRENCE DIXON

Landlord of the Champion of the Thames and former bookie, Lawrence Dixon reflects on the colourful cast of characters that inhabited his betting shops, the importance of service, and why swimming at Jesus Green Lido should be available on prescription.

ALTHOUGH I WAS born in Mill Road Maternity Hospital and grew up in Histon, my mother's roots were in Garden Walk, very close to Jesus Green Lido. My mum married young, my father was fresh out of the Army. He was a bookmaker, an alcoholic and a man about town. They had a volatile relationship and the marriage was never going to last long, so as children, my brother and I spent a lot of time with my grandmother in Garden Walk.

As kids we also spent a lot of time on Jesus Green. There was a putting green next to Jesus Green lock and there was Jesus Green Lido. We spent a lot of time at both so my brother and I were both good swimmers and good at putting.

Growing up, I always wanted to fly aeroplanes. My great hope was that one day, I'd go into space. I was enthralled by Yuri Gagarin and the space missions; we used to sit up and watch them on TV and that was a wonderful thing. I went to Mayfield Primary School, off Warwick Road. There was a baker's shop on the walk to school where we'd buy halfpenny rolls walking up to school.

At Mayfield I was always told, "you could definitely do better, Dixon." But I managed to fluke my 11-plus thanks to my grandfather. He had very poor breathing because he'd had tuberculosis when he was younger, although he still smoked big cigars. His doctor advised him to go and live by the sea, so he moved to Southend. When we visited him I'd read my father's old annuals and in one of them, there was a story about the children who lived on an island, and how they all escaped when it caught fire. I used that story to write my 11-plus – I figured the examiners would never have come across it.

Passing the 11-plus meant I went into the grammar stream at Impington Village College, but although I loved sport, other subjects bored me so I spent a lot of afternoons in the betting shop in Histon opposite the Railway View. Both my father and his dad Bob were bookmakers by trade, so by the mid-1970s it was a natural progression for me to go to work. University wasn't an option, my aspirations of being an airline pilot didn't get off the ground, and on my 18th birthday I got my bookmakers' licence.

We were interested in pitches in the dog racing world, so we travelled all over the place making the book. As youngsters we'd go to a flapping track – an unlicensed track – in Huntingdon. We also had a pitch at Cambridge City Football Club, which was also unlicensed initially. In the end, we had four betting shops: Victoria Road, Chesterton High Street, Milton Road and Chesterton Road near Mitcham's Corner.

As a working life, it was amazing, so much fun. Imagine the atmosphere of the best pub: Betting shops would trump that by miles, because everyone was in there to defeat us. Great wins were celebrated,

losses were generally speaking forgotten, but it was a great atmosphere. In those days you couldn't see across the betting shop for smoke. We had to open the doors every now and then and from the street you'd think the place was on fire for all the smoke billowing out.

We were very conscious of the customer, they were paramount to any success you had. Without them you were nothing.

Our stand on the dog track said "prompt payment and civility". Good manners were important to all my family, but to my grandfather in particular. He founded the betting shops, so we were always very mindful of him looking after our customers.

They were great days. Horse racing and dog racing took us all over the country. And we worked hard – I was up at six o'clock most mornings studying the form. My phone would be ringing at eight o'clock with people wanting to put bets on. And we'd work on the dog track. We did that four or five days a week, not getting home until 10 o'clock at night, but it was just fun, it was glorious.

When I started work in Chesterton High Street, the first wave of people would be pensioners or ladies bringing in their husband's bets. Then when the racing started in the afternoon, people would come in to listen. TVs weren't allowed in the shop but we had one in the back of the office and people would crowd into Bob Dixon's because they knew they could stand in the back.

Before off-track betting became legal in 1960, the shop in Chesterton High Street was called a veg shop. It had a bit of fruit in the window. But customers never came out with a banana, they always came out with a betting slip.

Illegal bookies were regularly raided by the police. They had to be seen to be doing something. Peggy Careless was a local lady of the night. She dressed in outlandishly bright colours and as she was a punter, the police would follow her to find bookies. She'd be easy to keep track of because she'd be wearing bright pink or orange. But we used to know

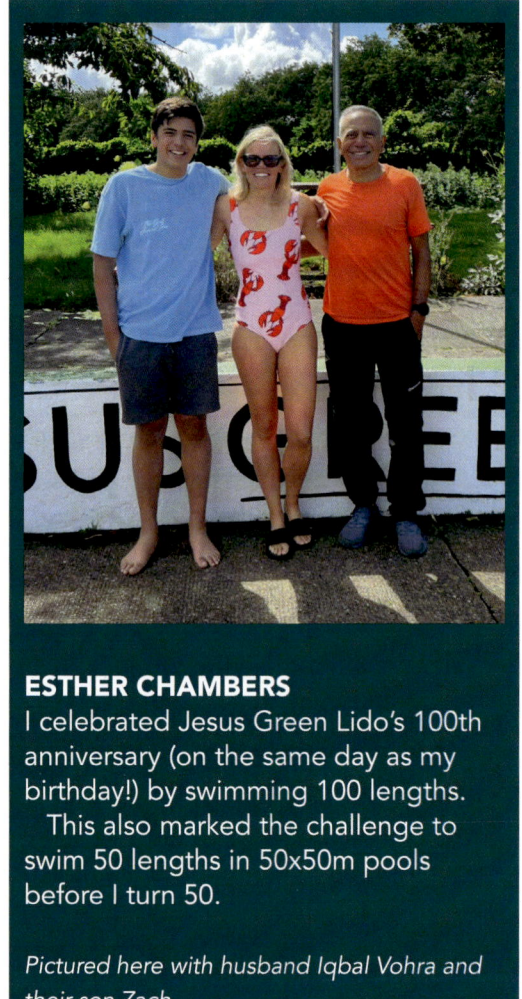

ESTHER CHAMBERS
I celebrated Jesus Green Lido's 100th anniversary (on the same day as my birthday!) by swimming 100 lengths.

This also marked the challenge to swim 50 lengths in 50x50m pools before I turn 50.

Pictured here with husband Iqbal Vohra and their son Zach

when the raids were coming because my uncle was a policeman. My grandfather would give someone five bob to stand in as bookmaker, they'd be arrested, taken down to the police station and then released.

The internet totally destroyed the aspects I concentrated on in betting shops. People started to wander away from the shops, betting on their phones or the internet. I could see it was a slippery slope, so I got out early. It had become stressful, my daughter was born, and I ended up buying the pub by mistake.

A friend – Nik Elmer – was a bricklayer, but fancied being involved in a pub after a lovely place to be: the beer has to be fantastic, the people who work with me are delightful, we just do what we do very well.

For me, swimming is headspace. And I like to think that in some small way it might help in my continuing battle with my weight. We were very privileged because when I was a child, Mayfield Primary School had a little swimming pool. I got my 14-yard certificate there. When I was at Impington Village College we'd swim at Parkside once a week. If we had enough money we'd get a packet of cheese and onion crisps and a bit of chocolate because we were always ravenous after swimming.

> **❝ For me, swimming is headspace. And I like to think that in some small way it might help in my continuing battle with my weight**

injuring his back. When the Champion of the Thames came on the market in 2000 we went to speak to Greene King about the procedure for getting a tenancy. While we were there, they offered him the pub but it was a substantial amount of money. I went to the dogs that night and won that amount of money so we took on the pub. We bought a second pub – the Rope & Twine (now the Punter).

The same thing's important to me in a pub as it was in the betting shops: service. I walk out of more pubs and restaurants than I stay in because I don't understand the concept of bad service. All we have is our customers. People come to the Champ because it's

As children, we'd try to jump over the fence to get into Jesus Green Lido without paying. And midnight swims were a thing when I was older. In the late 1970s we'd been in the Old Spring pub with my uncle Martin. He put up ten bob (50p) for the first one into Jesus Green Lido from the pub. There was a dash for the doors, people running up the street, and John the Co-op was first. But as he jumped in, he shouted "I can't swim." Martin went in to drag him out but lost his front teeth, which were false. And we spent quite a lot of time – spurred on by another reward – to get the teeth back.

The pool is a wonderful, wonderful community. Everyone's different shapes, sizes and abilities – a totally eclectic mix of people. But everyone has got a smile on their face because they're all there for the same reason.

I try to swim a mile, not very fast, but two or three times a week I try and do my 18 lengths. It's like when I used to play golf, it just clears your head, and the only thing you're interested in is not swallowing a leaf. You're aware of things, but you're not aware of things. And when you get out and sit down, someone says hello and suddenly you're having a conversation. You might have an ice cream. It just takes you away from all the rubbish that's occurring. It's such a benefit to people. Maybe it should be put on prescription.

For older people, swimming's an easy pastime, a good way of spending time on yourself. We don't spend enough time on ourselves. There's always someone else to do something for, and swimming is an individual thing. I see people swimming with earphones listening to music and I don't quite understand that. I don't want constant noise, I just want to be aware of the water and the birds.

I always had a hankering that at one stage – if things had been going really well – that I'd like to have taken over Jesus Green pool and turned it into what it should be. It's a fantastic space but I'd like it to be more accessible, better advertised. I'd get rid of the old changing rooms, and in a perfect world you could have a sliding roof, an area like a conservatory where people could have time for coffees and teas and lunch, and some heating – not hot, just 16C or 17C.

Cambridge is still essentially a university city, but it should be a wealthy enough city to be able to give more to its locals. There's probably a benefactor out there who might want to do something. It would be a great legacy. If I hadn't squandered all the money, I could even have been part of the plan!

SUZANNE DESMOND

SWIMMING AT THE Lido is unlike anywhere else in the world, the amount of joy felt swimming there is immeasurable, it is such a friendly and welcoming place.

The magical swims, be it sun, rain or snow. The exhilaration on completing your very first length when you swim there.

The joy in new people's faces, the screams and laughs when it is cold, the friends you make, the nods of hello to strangers in the winter bogged down with various bits of swimming kit on their way to or from a very cold swim. Ice-cream or hot chocolate?

Questions commonly heard at the Lido:
- How long is it? And how many lengths of a normal pool is that?
- How many lengths is a mile?
- How cold is it?
- How can you swim at that temperature?
- Where's Mary, I want ice cream?
- Why is it busy on a Sunday morning?
- How much for the lockers?
- Annie, what's that song you are singing?
- Ooh I like your costume, where did you get it?
- Where's Mary, I want a bacon butty?
- How many people can fit into the sauna (I mean really, it's like the TARDIS)?
- Did you know it is 100 years old?

Sara prepares for her synchro show, and, below, Andy Bonnett's drawing of lifeguard Cory

SARA LEDWITH

AS A STUDENT, though based just around the corner, I was oblivious to it. Decades later we brought our then-toddler Cory on a sunny day. So many trees shaded the pool. It was cold. I think he cried.

Post menopause, looking for ways to lift the spirits, I found it to be a paradise. In winter I would gaze through fence and brambles at the green sludge where my happiness was held prisoner.

Then came winter opening. I now visit as much as I can. I breathe better at Jesus Green. People are nicer here. Our then-toddler is a lifeguard.

SAM THOROGOOD

Throughout the winter, Sam Thorogood organises Serotonin Swims at Jesus Green Lido, providing a safe, inclusive community for new and seasoned swimmers to discover the benefits of cold water. Swimming at Jesus Green Lido, he says, has been the good friend he's turned to when times are tough.

WHEN WAS THE last time someone made you feel appreciated, when someone noticed how hard you've been trying? How do you cope when you're in pain, when your body hurts or thoughts feel overwhelming?

The idea behind Serotonin Swim is to give people a convenient answer to both these important questions. Jesus Green Lido is famous for its warm and inclusive community. The science of cold water swimming is becoming equally famous for how it helps lift mood and reduce inflammation. All we needed to do was bring these two things together, which led to the launch of Serotonin Swim in October 2022.

The premise was simple: give people recognition for swimming one length or more, and share tips and techniques to help people adjust to cold water swimming. Over 90 people turned up to the first Serotonin Swim. Since then, more than 480 people have attended a Serotonin Swim at Jesus Green Lido. From 'I just feel better after a swim' and 'this is the highlight of my week' to 'this has helped me in more ways than I can explain,' the feedback has been overwhelming.

REBECCA TAYLOR

People, leaves, rain. Jesus Green Lido is just different. I love the encouragement and friendship offered by strangers as we prepare to enter the water in winter. The intense cold brings about a rush of joy and sense of achievement.

In autumn the leaves falling through the water land on us, creating daft adornments which demand a silly photo or two.

All year round the sun hitting the pool floor looks magical, especially on grey days when it wasn't expected. I smile watching the pretty waveforms on the bottom and sides of the pool. It's my number one place of happiness and calm.

In my day job I help support people's mental wellbeing – from surgeons, nurses and teachers to administrators, scientists and business leaders. What does everyone I meet have in common? Everyone is looking to find simple ways to help them manage difficult thoughts and focus more effectively.

Swimming is the single most effective technique I know to bring these benefits in the shortest time. Swimming brings our attention to the present as effectively as any meditation or mindfulness practice I've experienced. Swimming improves mood by increasing the feel-good hormone serotonin. Swimming improves our response to stress – physical movement helps strengthen our resilience.

A swim can be a quick jump in and out of the water. It can be one length, 1km or more. The most important benefits are the ones you experience. Science is a useful guide but personal experience is better.

Join serotoninswim.org and experience something that might just help your life in the way it helped mine: from coping with my mum's cancer to children born into intensive care, swimming at Jesus Green Lido has been the good friend I've turned to when times are tough.

SARAH BLOWER

I WORKED AS a lifeguard at Jesus Green Lido and Abbey pool between 1992 and 1998. My first impression was that the pool was very long and very cold!

I remember having a photo taken by the *Cambridge Evening News* of me bursting out of the water on the pool's first day of opening in summer. The water was about 14C but it took my breath away.

Now, I swim here all year, three times a week. I'm generally a wetsuit swimmer (not all year, mind you). I prefer swimming here in spring and autumn when the pool is less busy and doesn't taste of suncream, although it is great seeing how busy it gets in the hot summer months.

Unless it's raining, I get ready by the benches outside the ladies' changing rooms nearest the heated hut. I start swimming at the end by the pump room, usually in the middle lane. It really throws me if friends I swim with suggest changing on the grass.

When I started swimming again at Jesus Green a couple of years ago, one of the first people I bumped into who I remember from when I worked here was Nicky Blanning. She hasn't changed one bit! There are lots of faces I recognise and some names I remember: Alex Buxton, Mary Williams, Diana Beddow, Annie Morgan James.

There are so many things to love about the pool. The people who swim here make it special, but it's mainly the sense of calm it brings. You could be having the most stressful day and yet when you go through the turnstiles all those worries seem to go away.

GUARDIAN ANGELS

FINN BARNES

Lifeguard Finn Barnes has been working at the Lido on and off for five years. It 'soothes his chakra'.

I ENJOY WORKING with most of my colleagues. It is a fun place of business. I appreciate being outside as this soothes my chakra. I also enjoy meeting new customers, conversing with the regulars and gardening. It's a privilege to watch the seasons come and go and sweep leaves.

It is also a very intense job. Last summer one of our customers had a cardiac arrest in the changing rooms. Together with my colleagues Freya Standing and Melissa Green, we used a defibrillator to restart his heart. The paramedics arrived and took him to hospital. He remained in hospital for a week, but was discharged. That was an uncomfortable but gratifying day at the pool.

The diversity of trees around the pool is impressive. The atmosphere of the pool during the quieter winter months, and the energy of the summer months make it special.

No one day is the same, and that makes the job exhilarating.

GABRIELE SCARMATTO

Gabriele Scarmatto lifeguarded at Jesus Green Lido between spring 2021 and autumn 2023. He loves the pool because working there enables him to be immersed in nature, because of its generous community, and because it has echoes of his native Sicily.

WHEN I FIRST saw the pool, it reminded me of being surrounded by water. I am from Sicily, and I am used to the sound of water around me, so the Lido reminds me of my hometown, Sant Agata di Militello.

The weather you get used to here, and it can be colder working outside, but with the right equipment and clothes people can climb Everest or go to the Arctic. It's not a big issue – it's not as if it's minus 50C.

Working outside means lots of sunlight and lots of vitamin D; I love that. And fresh air rather than in an indoor pool where you breathe chlorine. At Jesus Green you breathe oxygen from the grass and trees and you're surrounded by sounds of nature – the wind, the birds. It's much better and more relaxing and I prefer it here.

The first winter, the early weeks were a bit stressful. When the water temperature dropped below 10C, some people stayed in the pool too long and a few collapsed outside the pool as they weren't used to the cold water. As lifeguards, we're trained to deal with such events and managed everything well, and by late November it improved as the regular winter swimmers were prepared and knew when to stop.

Gabriele soaking up the vitamin D while on lifeguard duty

The second winter saw even more people swimming. We made several improvements to the facilities. We created the 'Snug', a small heated space where people can enjoy a coffee or one of Mary's toasties and keep warm. It was an old container full of disused vending machines, now it's a lovely community space, and the sauna has been fixed.

Every year we try to make improvements – from new compost bins for the leaves to new matting to prevent people from slipping in icy conditions. We're always trying to make little adjustments and improvements.

In winter, the last hour's swimming from 6 o'clock, when the sky's dark and the lights are on, is a different swimming experience and very popular. It would be good to have swimming sessions later in the evening in the summer, around 9 or 10 o'clock in August with clear skies, the moon and stars. If the days are warm, the pool retains heat even when the temperature drops during the evening. I think it'd be very popular.

I love Jesus Green pool because I am surrounded by nature; it doesn't feel like being in the city, it feels like being in the countryside. I love the customers and the community, people show their gratitude. Here, people ask how you are and say thank you. People are friendly and happier than in the indoor pools – it's different.

I love my job – keeping things tidy, talking to the customers, making improvements. I love it when people come here for the first time and say, "Wow, it's so beautiful." My main goal is to make a great experience for the customers. It feels like my little aquarium, my little garden that I must look after and keep nice and tidy, but on a huge scale.

My favourite season is the winter because of all the regulars, the loyal customers who are always happy, friendly and glad the pool is open. We provide a service for them. By keeping the pool open during winter we complete the full circle. It can be tough, but the swimmers appreciate it. We are pushing the bar, opening even when it is snowing, the customers are still coming, and they are thankful, which is rewarding.

And we have an amazing team of lifeguards. We all help each other, and we have Mary running the cafe. She's great with people, she looks after us, providing hot drinks and help. Together, we have an amazing team spirit.

KANE SMITH

Lifeguard, photographer and former competitive swimmer Kane Smith explains what makes Jesus Green Lido special, working with a community of winter swimmers, and what he's trying to capture in his photographs of the pool.

I STARTED WORKING here in May 2021. During Lockdown, I saw a post on Twitter hiring lifeguards for Jesus Green Lido. I applied, did all the interviews remotely and my lifeguarding course finished the day Lockdown ended.

I'd been inside for nearly two years because of Covid, and wanted a job which was outside, sociable and in a nice part of Cambridge, so the Lido made sense. And lifeguarding made sense because I'd been a competitive swimmer – Freestyle and Butterfly, 50m and 100m, at university and national level – and love the water.

Although I grew up near Linton, just outside Cambridge, I only came to the Lido twice as a child. But I remember thinking that it was strange to change outside, and that the pool was green and full of leaves. When I started work here the pool was blue, the water was clear and my first impression was how calm and peaceful it is.

Training as a lifeguard was in a noisy, hectic, indoor pool. Although I sometimes work at Parkside, I prefer Jesus Green because it's quiet and tranquil, and even when it's busy it's a relaxing place.

Working the first winter the pool was open was difficult because some swimmers weren't familiar with cold water swimming and stayed in too long. Although we're trained to deal with hypothermia, it's important to track people in the pool and be alert to the possibility. We know the regulars and how many lengths they usually swim. During the second winter, people were better prepared, and lifeguarding was less stressful.

Winter customers are a different breed of people. You get to know the winter regulars better because there are fewer people at the pool, and you talk to them more. Most people who swim here in winter also swim in the summer. Winter customers tend to be better swimmers – more competent, more confident and more patient – and they kind of own the pool. Pilvi Saarikoski swims long distances freestyle all winter. When it's 6C they might be the only person in the fast lane – it's their lane and they kind of own it.

My favourite time of the year is coming

out of winter into spring. The pool is still quiet, the water's still cold, so we still have our hardy swimmers who know what they're doing. You're still lifeguarding them, but it's not as intense as lifeguarding children and young adults. The weather is starting to pick up and you can get some lovely days in spring. As soon as the leaves appear on the trees again, the place has a completely different feel from the winter – it's more enclosed.

I've always wanted to run a swimming pool because I swam so much as a child and saw how it was done. Jesus Green Lido is a unique pool and community; it has the potential to be excellent. What I

> **The lifeguard team all love the Lido and appreciate what it is – something special**

like most is trying to improve the place so the pool can reach its potential. The team here is unique too; we all love the Lido and appreciate what it is – something special. As a result, the teamwork's more cohesive. We enjoy it more and there's a great sense of attachment.

I swim in the summer and the coldest I've swum here out of choice is 13C. It's a unique pool to swim in. Because I used to swim competitively I'm used to 25m pools and 25m splits. Here it's completely different, and you have to ignore all that and enjoy your swimming. In summer, all the lifeguards swim between shifts or jump in to cool down before getting back to lifeguarding. Val Moore is the only lifeguard who swims regularly in winter. We'll go in when there's a milestone. When it was 1C – the coldest we've ever seen it and there was ice on the water – Finn Barnes and I had a dip simply to see what it was like.

A hot topic of conversation among the staff is, 'If you had an unlimited budget for Jesus Green Lido, what would you do?' I would want to keep the aesthetic, the feeling of the place but refurbish it sympathetically. I'd make the pool deck level – so the water comes level to the sides – which would make it easier to keep clean, and introduce pool covers. It is hard to keep on top of because it's 100 yards long. I once painted the free boards – the white and red bit around the pool. It took me two days to do 20 yards. By the time you're finished it's almost time to start doing it again!

Leisure centres all have cafes, but Jesus Green isn't like other leisure centres because the cafe here is such an integral part of the community. Some people come here just to talk to Mary. She is a little part of the community and so is the cafe.

Photography is my hobby and I take lots of photos of the pool. It's very long, very thin and unique – it's the only one like it in the world – so capturing it in photos is very tricky. And because of its age there's a lot of history in the photos; Trying to capture the feeling of the pool, the impression it makes when you first walk in isn't easy. I love seeing people when they see the pool for the first time – when they walk past reception and open their mouths in amazement and wonder.

GEORGE PEMBERTON

George Pemberton, who was lifeguarding when the Lido introduced winter swimming in 2021, talks about the contrasting working days of summer and winter and dreams of new changing rooms, a new reception area and new cafe.

What made you start lifeguarding?
To be honest, it was something I thought would look good on my CV. But after I started lifeguarding, they offered me a job because pools are always crying out for lifeguards.

I started lifeguarding when I was 16 and began working for Better a year later. When I was 18 and finished college I came over to Jesus Green Lido full-time and started my first season here as a lifeguard.

Tell us about your first session at Jesus Green Lido.

When Better mentioned there was an outdoor pool in Cambridge I decided to check it out. What they didn't mention was that it was unheated and that I'd have to test all my skills in the pool. That was quite a shock.

When I first came down here before the season started in 2017 it was 8C. We were supposed to go into the water wearing tracksuit bottoms and a jumper so I turned up wearing tracksuit bottoms and a jumper. Nobody told me to bring a spare set of clothes, so I brought swimwear and a T-shirt. Being a naive 18-year-old I didn't say anything, went into the water with what I was wearing and had to walk home in my swim stuff looking like a right doughnut!

What's the best part about lifeguarding at Jesus Green?

Being outside and working with customers every day. The customers here are probably the best customers you'll ever deal with at a swimming pool in the UK. We've got a really great community.

How does it differ from working at an indoor pool?

The community is completely different. There's a different feel about the place. Being outside and having fresh air is a world away from being in a stuffy indoor environment. You can see it in the staff here – they all love working here compared to lifeguarding at an indoor pool.

You have to have a certain personality to work here, because you're so much closer to the customers. At other pools you can just turn up and do your job.

Here, you have to be talking to and engaging with customers all the time.

After the third lockdown in 2021 when we reopened early, in April, I made a real effort to learn all our swimmers' names. A lot of staff followed suit and I think it makes a real difference.

What was it like moving to year-round opening?

We'd known it was coming for a while. During Covid we explored the options, surveyed the swimmers and finally decided to take the plunge.

The first winter was really good, but the winter of 2022/23 was brutal. The pool froze over, which we didn't have the year before because it was a mild winter. So we had ice to contend with, but it's all part of the fun of working here. It's another thing you wouldn't get at other pools in the UK.

How's lifeguarding different in winter and summer?

Keeping warm on poolside is definitely one big challenge. But the good news is only working four or five hours, because opening hours are compressed. That's better than working 12 or 13 hour days in summer.

We're fully trained in dealing with hypothermia and cold water shock and we had extra staff on board. Briefing swimmers on cold water swimming has been interesting. We work with our Swim Doctor Colin who runs sessions for swimmers new to cold water swimming. The sauna's been great for people to warm up in, but we've still had to take care of some people in the first aid room to re-warm them.

On crazy hot days in the summer you have more to deal with poolside. When

Better staff Chris Green, George Pemberton, Stephen Rayment and Gabriele Scarmatto

we have 1,000 people at the Lido it can put a strain on lifeguards, but it's one of the highlights of working here. Personally, I love the mayhem. I enjoy it when it's really busy. They're the kind of days I thrive on because at the end of the day you get a huge sense of achievement, having made a positive difference to so many people's days.

What do you think the Lido might be like in 25 years' time?

I hope the nature of the pool never changes because that's the foundation of the community here. But I'd love to see some investment and building work – new changing rooms, a new reception area, a new cafe. There needs to be a sensitive mix of old and new.

I'd like to see the length of the pool preserved, and the greenery, because there's nothing else like it in the UK. It's been part of Cambridge's heritage for 100 years.

DARYL EMES

Daryl Emes, Partnership Manager for Better in Cambridge talks about the joys and challenges of operating Jesus Green Lido, what it means to be a social enterprise, and his vision for the next 100 years.

Tell us a bit about your job?

As Partnership Manager for Better in Cambridge, I have overall responsibility for all Better's facilities in the city. I'm also the conduit between Cambridge City Council and the leisure facilities we operate. It's my job to ensure that what we deliver is what the Council wants.

I've worked for Better for 20 years. I started on the graduate scheme in 2003. After working at partnerships and centres in London, I came to Cambridge when Better was awarded the contract in 2013.

Better is the UK's largest leisure social enterprise. What's that mean?

Social enterprises are businesses which trade for a social or environmental purpose. There are more than 100,000 social enterprises in the UK, contributing £60 billion to the economy and employing around two million people.

Social enterprises demonstrate a better way to do business, one that prioritises benefit to people and planet and uses the majority of any profit to further their mission. Social enterprises contribute to reducing economic inequality, improving social justice and to environmental sustainability.

Working for a social enterprise matches my ethos. The structure of the organisation, the not-for-profit angle, and the fact it reinvests its profits into the community was a big pull for me. These values were central to GLL when it was set up in 1993, and Better (as it's now known) lives and breathes them still. Everything we do is for the communities in which we work – trying to make the facilities better and make the programmes we offer more accessible.

What does that mean for those communities?

Our vision is that leisure centres become hubs for the community, that communities feel some ownership of them and so they deliver added benefits over and above good pools, gyms and leisure facilities.

There are many operators in the UK which provide leisure services. We want to do better. Our challenge is to deliver added benefits to the people and communities we serve. Of course we want to run great leisure centres, but we're also always asking ourselves what more we can do to create pathways for people to use our facilities throughout their lives.

Why do you think widening participation in exercise is so important?

I grew up with sport. I don't mean team games or elite competition but health, fitness and wellbeing. It brings so many positives. Sport genuinely improves people's mood, boosts wellbeing, fosters social interaction, and means people remain mobile and independent much later in life. All those things matter. We are, and should be, at the heart of that.

Jesus Green Lido is a great example. It gives people time in nature, in water and in a community. Jesus Green Lido's a community for everyone, from first-time

users to people who swim every day, twice a day, or even three times a day.

Our 100-yard pool means everyone is literally in it together, regardless of how well you swim. From the minute you walk in, Jesus Green Lido feels welcoming, and people feel part of something. If someone wants to come twice in July to sit on the side of the pool during hot weather, that's just as lovely as people coming every day.

What's challenging about operating a lido like Jesus Green?

Operating a lido is very different to an indoor pool. There are two sides to that, as far as Jesus Green's concerned. Until 2021 it was a seasonal facility. Now we're open year-round, it's very different to manage.

When it was open from May to September it was rather boom and bust. We'd spend two months in spring cleaning the place and getting it ready for opening. Recruiting seasonal staff was always challenging because you could only offer them five or six months' work and many people don't work like that.

Our climate obviously makes operating outdoors challenging. The UK loves a forecast, particularly in the build-up to a heat wave. Stories in the media about Cambridge being hotter than Spain create huge anticipation – you can feel the Lido getting ready for what it does best. You can feel the excitement in the air because you're thinking 'here we go!' Then the heat arrives and you get walloped for three or four days because when it's 30C in Cambridge, everyone wants to be at Jesus Green Lido. Managing 300 people in the pool and 500 people around the pool is a different proposition.

Year-round opening has removed some of those challenges. Staffing has become easier because the Lido has a core team supplemented by casual staff. Year-round opening has to some extent smoothed out that boom and bust.

What made Better take the plunge into being open all year?

Covid certainly had an impact, but it was in my mind before then. Outdoor swimming was really taking off, we learned a lot from West Reservoir in Hackney, and new technology helped. It seemed like a good opportunity.

Other pools are now asking us to share

> ❝ I don't believe it could revert to being a seasonal pool, because it's so popular and well supported

our experience. Many are thinking that if Jesus Green Lido can do it, we can too. I think many more outdoor pools will extend their seasons.

Jesus Green Lido must be one of the oldest facilities Better manages; is it seen as a millstone or a jewel in the crown?

My job involves travelling and meeting other Partnership Managers up and down the UK and everyone always asks about Jesus Green Lido. They will have visited hundreds of other pools and leisure centres but Jesus Green sticks in everyone's minds.

Better's structure is a bit like the John Lewis Partnership. All the staff have shared ownership of the social enterprise, we each have one share and one vote. So we organise several staff events each year, including cycling London to Cambridge. That finishes on Jesus Green so we always have a staff BBQ at the Lido. As a result, everyone at Better is interested in its future; it's very much valued as a jewel in the crown.

Ice caused some consternation in the winter of 2022/23. West Reservoir doesn't freeze so we couldn't ask them for advice. It's something unique to the Lido that we now need to deal with, and we did. But the fabric of the building's not completely set up for year-round use because it was built as a seasonal pool.

What do you think Jesus Green Lido could be like in 25 years' time?

I think it'll be very different. I don't believe it could revert to being a seasonal pool, because it's so popular and well supported.

I think it needs a new entrance and new indoor changing facilities at one end of the pool with a cafe that also serves the play park.

Having created a year-round pool, we need to provide some indoor space for both customers and staff. It could be a wonderful community space, somewhere for exhibitions as well as exercise classes and something that would enable us to really expand the programme we offer.

On the pool itself, I'm an advocate of its length. It's one of the things that makes it iconic. But the pool needs a different profile – it needs to be shallower for longer. If it was 0.9 metres deep for 15-20 metres it would be much better for families. And I'd love to see something for younger visitors, like a splash pad.

What are the obstacles to major improvements?

Funding, as ever. We're talking millions of pounds. I think the political will exists to do it, but the Council faces funding challenges on all fronts.

Jesus Green needs several million pounds to future-proof it. We might be able to change the pool's profile and raise it to deck level, which would make it easier to remove leaves in the autumn, with a 10-15 year contract. But something much longer would be needed to deliver a new building. Charlton Lido – where we have a 99-year lease – shows what can be achieved with longer contracts.

Why is Jesus Green so special for so many people?

It gives people a sense of belonging, regardless of where they're from and what they're about. There's something about it that fits people's psyche – people feel comfortable there.

There's huge camaraderie there. People get a sense of support. It's a place where everyone genuinely wants others to have a good time. That's its place in the community. And all sorts of people from Cambridge and further afield enjoy it – poolside is always a real smorgasbord of people.

Some people say that not enough children use it. Are you kidding me? I see hundreds there every summer, coming down after school to meet friends, chat and have a swim.

In December 2022, Jesus Green Lido won the World Cup of Pools. What did you make of that?

It was hilarious, mainly because I'd never heard of it. But it became exceptionally competitive, something that shows people's feelings about Jesus Green Lido. People feel a sense of ownership and have a vested interest in it; it's part of them. That's great because it's what we want as a social enterprise but is something that can be hard to foster. People here feel they have a stake in Jesus Green Lido.

The World Cup of Pools showed a sheer bloody-mindedness to win that was indicative of the community. We wanted to prove to everyone that our Lido – and our community – was the best. It reflected the spirit of the place, what it means to people, and showed everyone our place in the lido world.

And do you ever get to enjoy it?

My kids love it. And I treasure the times after work when I have time to do a couple of lengths and sit on the side with a book. But it's hard, because I never feel off duty. Over the years I've thought that I will truly enjoy Jesus Green Lido when I'm no longer Partnership Manager. I can't wait to come here as someone with a shared history with the pool but who isn't on duty!

IAN ROSS and JULIE DURRANT

Julie Durrant and Ian Ross work together at Cambridge City Council's Leisure Services department but first met working at the City's swimming pools. Here, they reminisce about rainy days, roast dinners and how the pool survived the wave of lido closures that swept the UK in the 1980s.

Julie: I was born at the Rosie Hospital and brought up in Cambridge. My first job was as Ian's early morning cleaner at Abbey Pool alongside my studies, and when I was 17 I trained to be a lifeguard. I've been the admin manager for all the pools in Cambridge, and from 1993 to 2005 I worked for Empire Leisure and SLM Everyone Active (the private operators who ran the city's pools) before moving to the City Council's sport and recreation team. So Ian's been my manager for a long time, he can't get away from me.

Ian: I was born at home in Cherry Hinton and apart from a few wilderness

years in Pontypridd, Wales, where I went to college, I've lived and worked in Cambridge all my life. Because I've got a background in surveying, my first job was drawing up maps and plans of all the city's pools, but I've had a whole range of jobs, from custodian at Abbey Pool and lifeguarding at Jesus Green Lido to deputy contracts manager for Empire Leisure before moving to the City Council, where I'm now Community, Sport & Recreation Manager.

The best bit of the job is the variety. We do everything from building and development projects to working with user groups, including the Friends of Jesus Green Lido, trying to understand and help deliver what the public wants.

Julie: Because we've always lived in Cambridge, working with the pools feels like looking after assets that belong to us. Jesus Green Lido has a special place in our hearts.

My mum owned the chip shop on Newmarket Road for many years. My dad passed away when I was only seven years old, so my granddad played a pivotal role in our lives. He lived in Carlyle Road, just opposite Jesus Green, so when he was looking after us we'd often spend all afternoon swimming at the pool.

As a child, the pool seemed huge. In those days there were no limits on bather loads; the place was so full you'd have to walk over people. Granddad would give us a few pounds for ice creams, and if you wanted to go out to buy one the lifeguards would stamp your hand so you could get back in.

I was the most envied lifeguard at Jesus

Green Lido. In the summer, we'd work from 10am to 8pm. My granddad always cooked a roast on Sundays. He'd put it in the oven and then go to the NCI (New Chesterton Institute) for a few drinks. Then he'd plate me up a Sunday dinner and bring it down to the pool for me. Everyone was so jealous – especially if it was pouring with rain and there were only the ducks to lifeguard.

Ian: My earliest memories of Jesus Green Lido come from my mum. She went to Brunswick School and used to come to the Lido for her swimming lessons. They had a love-hate relationship with the place, having had to learn how to swim in cold water; it was never a place she associated with fun and enjoyment.

I got to know the pool when I started working here. We'd start in February and drain the pool. Seeing its transformation from murky green water full of litter to a glittering pool was great. In those days we had no pressure washers, instead we used an old fireman's hose with an antiquated brass nozzle. When you turned it on you'd really have to hold those hoses otherwise you'd be flung around the pool.

Julie: Lifeguarding at Jesus Green was the best: If you were a good lifeguard, and you did your cleaning, your reward was to come and work at the Lido. My best friends Emma and Kate, we'd been at school together since we were 11 years old, both lifeguarded too. And this is where I met my partner Leigh. He'd come to help out in the basket room because his best mate Ben was also a lifeguard here. He didn't get paid, but he ended up with me – a much bigger prize! My younger brother Ed also worked at the pool for a number of years and stars in the Jesus Green movie.

Ian: Having those three on shift was a nightmare for any duty manager because they were the best of friends. It was difficult to control them sometimes, and get them to walk round the pool separately rather than standing together talking. Then in the evening, before closing, you'd have to wait for them to get glammed up to go into town.

Julie: The community of swimmers here became particularly strong when there were concerns that the Lido might close and Alex Buxton set up the Friends of Jesus Green Lido.

Ian: It was a time of council cuts and changes, and there was a proposal that we might look at either shortening the season or closing the pool altogether. It was at a time when the UK lost dozens of lidos. The Friends started as a lobbying group, we built up a good working relationship and they've always helped local politicians realise that the pool means a lot to local people.

Since then, councillors of all the political parties have been keen to be seen to support Jesus Green Lido, and over the past three years they've been very supportive of keeping the pool open during the winter. Everyone's recognised outdoor swimming is about more than a life skill, recreation and physical activity – it's about mental health and community too. Covid was a particular period that showed again the real value of a pool like this.

I think Jesus Green Lido survived because Cambridge had contracted out its leisure services relatively early on. That

meant Jesus Green Lido was difficult to remove from these contracts and the other pools helped generate profits to help sustain it. We also had a large catchment area: our nearest pools were at Peterborough, an hour's drive, and other outdoor pools such as Broomhill (in Ipswich) have since closed.

Julie: And Jesus Green was never complicated. We'd open in summer, you could come and swim, sunbathe and enjoy yourself, and then we'd close at the end of the season in September.

One of my favourite times of day at the Lido is early morning when no one else is here.

You'd done your leaf sweeping, you'd look out across Jesus Green at people getting on with their lives, and the pool felt like a secret place, it felt very peaceful. Once you opened up, it'd be really busy if it was hot, but if the weather was bad you'd have one swimmer and a duck. Sometimes we'd not take any cash all day, as the only swimmers were season ticket holders. We knew all the season ticket holders – the core of the community – people like Terry Gorham. I can't think of Jesus Green without thinking of Terry, and Arthur Mansfield.

Ian: There was a cast of characters, often with nicknames like Smiley Mary. In the late 1980s and early 90s on sunny days the place was heaving, you'd have to tiptoe over people to lifeguard. It was so busy that people had to put their towels down on the edge of the pool and sit with their feet in the water.

Julie: On those hot summer days people would scramble to lay their towels out at the pump room end to save a space. People would arrive in the morning, bring a picnic and stay all day. We'd have to look out for alcohol and gently remind women that they weren't allowed to sunbathe topless.

Ian: The place is showing its age. The plant, the pool tank and other equipment needs upgrading. Over coming years we'll examine how best to do that, perhaps by re-profiling the pool so that we have a larger, shallower area for families to enjoy. And perhaps bring the water up to deck level, which would make it easier to keep the water free of leaves. We might add a thermal lining and pool covers, but the pool will probably never be heated, it's just too large a volume of water.

Our longer-term aspiration is for a new entrance building that would house changing rooms, toilets and reception as well as a cafe and community space. Unfortunately, because the pool is simply a 100-year-old pool tank without art deco buildings that were built at Peterborough and elsewhere, it doesn't tick the right boxes for Heritage Lottery funding.

Julie: I'd like to see more families with young children being able to enjoy the pool. It'd be nice to have a little splash zone for them.

Ian: The amount of capital investment, which is what the pool needs now, is a challenge. It's something we're actively investigating. We need to invest much more heavily in the facility so it's here for another 100 years. That's our aim and will hopefully be our legacy – leaving the pool as a fabulous facility that's used by everybody.

COLIN CAMPBELL

Swim teacher, open water swimming coach and cold water advocate, whether it's sunny and hoaching or empty and dreich.

AT THE TIME of writing, I've been coaching at Jesus Green Lido for two years. Most Monday mornings and evenings since autumn 2021, I've roamed the pool side with my Swim Doctor T-shirt on, observing swimmers and offering advice to anyone who'll listen. A few of them are in this book.

Often, a small tweak can make a big difference to your stroke. A shift in head or hand position. A greater awareness of your body position, hip roll or kick. A more relaxed exhalation. Other times, you have to put the lengths in, and there's a cohort of inspiring swimmers at the Lido who do just that.

I get profound satisfaction from swim teaching and swim coaching. Being able to help swimmers at the Lido improve their technique, confidence and open water safety has been one of the best things about moving to Cambridge.

When we moved here from Scotland in 2021 I'd left behind a vibrant swim coaching business and community. In and around Edinburgh, Fife and East Lothian I'd coached more than 200 adults, helping folk of all abilities safely embrace the joy of open water swimming. I'd taught a similar number of children as a swim teacher with Edinburgh Leisure.

So it was hard leaving all that behind. With false optimism I told my friends, Och, the sea's not that far away (it is though) and I can swim in the River Cam (I prefer not to), and there're a few lakes nearby (they're all tiny).

Prior to moving, I'd swum in the sea pretty much every day for two years, through several winters, and while I missed the salt water and the Firth of Forth's generally gentle ebb and flood, it was the community and my friends I missed most.

And so, by way of the lifeguards and the folk I see here, I've felt myself become part of another community. Smiles and hellos have evolved to shared tales and forming friendships. Swimming lessons have given way to life stories. I'm approached for tips or advice, and gladly share them. In truth, I can't help myself offering advice even when unasked for (sorry if I ever overstep).

The Lido will never replace the big open water swims I yearn for, but coaching in this magnificent pool, whether it's sunny and hoaching or empty and dreich, has and continues to be a great pleasure and a real privilege.

MARY COTTON

Much loved for her hot chocolate, her toasties, and her warm welcome, Mary is a Jesus Green Lido legend. Here, she talks about what the pool has meant to her through childhood, pregnancy and breast cancer, about its many moods, its community, and why – after swimming for more than 40 years – she decided to learn front crawl in earnest.

JESUS GREEN LIDO is my favourite place in the world, I love it. It's somewhere everyone is smiley and friendly. Life would be awful without the pool – it gives you energy, it gives you peace and it just perks up your day. Before I started working at the Lido in 2018, swimming here would be the highlight of my morning.

The Lido has so many moods: I love it when it rains, because lots of people get out but it is wonderful in the rain; I love it in the dark; I love it even when it's grey but I prefer it when it's sunny. It gives me joy and tranquillity. It's a routine, something you do every day, you just get in the water and swim.

I've swum at Jesus Green Lido over the years with my grandparents, parents, siblings, husband and children. I first came when I was six or seven with my brother, sister and father and I thought it was amazing. My grandparents lived in Great Shelford, and we would spend our summer holidays there and, particularly on rainy days, we would come to Jesus Green in the Land Rover and swim. I used to have an old photograph of me diving off the diving boards.

My father was a schoolmaster at

Mary Cotton has helped revive many cold swimmers with her hot drinks and warm welcome

Charterhouse. I learned to swim there because they had a pool, so I was always able to swim. After university, when I was 21, I came back to live with my grandmother and I'd swim at Jesus Green in my lunch breaks and after work. That was around 1990, when you could get 10-swim cards and season tickets. Throughout my 20s I'd swim here all summer, but not as much as I swim now.

I remember swimming at Jesus Green when I was pregnant and then bringing my baby, Ben. He was born in May, so I would have brought him here from June. I would walk from Ross Street, where we live, and spend the day here with my baby. He slept in the pushchair and the lifeguards would keep an eye on him. I'd swim up and down doing breaststroke not very fast and if he woke, they would tell me. I'd have a picnic and have a lot of nappies lined up – we used real nappies – and chat to other mothers.

When I used to come in my 30s, before I worked here, I didn't know that many people. I would smile at people, but didn't sit and chat and that's changed since I have been working here. It's such a great community; people are always friendly, but it's not intrusive. If you just want to come and sit, that's fine, you don't get bothered – it's a great place to come and exercise and hang out. I would always be sad when the pool closed in September, and I always counted the days until it opened again the following year.

One of the major changes for me was when I started working here five years ago and became part of the team, but the biggest change has been having the pool open in the winter. This is my second year of swimming through the winter. The first year I didn't know if I could do it, but we just kept going. There is such a community at Jesus Green, so

when the opening hours were restricted I got together with some people to swim in the river. Since then, I've just continued swimming in cold water, this year swimming more in the pool. I just think it's fantastic, I love swimming in cold water. Recently, I decided that I don't enjoy it when it's below 5C, but I still do it! At the moment it's 8C – I love 8C – it just makes you feel amazing.

In 2019, my second year working at Jesus Green, I was diagnosed with breast cancer. The biopsy meant I couldn't swim on the opening day in May, and I couldn't swim for six weeks, but working here was important. I had to wait again to go back into the water after I had my mastectomy. They said wait six weeks, but after four and a half weeks I showed my friend and she said I could go in. I just wanted to be in the water; you're supported in the water and I love being in the water, particularly when it is sunny. You go under the water, it's the most immersive and amazing experience.

Last winter I was obsessed with swimming every day but this winter I've been more relaxed about it because I know I can do it. It gives you time to breathe. I often swim with my friend Cath and we chat, but I also swim on my own. In the winter I make sure I have tons of layers, two pairs of socks, tights, trousers. I've got a dryrobe and a hat and I get changed in the first aid room, it's like a mini sauna of my own.

I've recently taken up front crawl. I put in my earplugs and my hat on and then I'm in my own world. The last length I take my goggles off so I can just appreciate it – this morning it was beautiful – the trees and the sky. If you're on your back kicking you can see the choppiness of the water, it's just beautiful. And I like going under water. Today I noticed with my ear plugs that it's all muffled. In the summer you hear the children laughing and splashing and the sounds of people having fun.

Breaststroke I like because you've

got your head out and you can take it all in. But I like front crawl because I hadn't done it before and it's important to learn new things when you're older – and because it's faster. I used to find it tiring because I held my breath under water but now I'm working on my stroke with Colin the Swim Doctor. He always focuses on one thing. Today, it was that I stop kicking when I breathe, so that's something to improve. That makes you forget you're exercising.

My husband used to be a swimmer but not in cold water. He loves Jesus Green Lido because of its length but it has to be about 19C. One of my children was a lifeguard here last summer but he didn't really get on with it; he was 16 and too young to enjoy the after-work social scene of going to the pub. My other son Tom is looking forward to being a lifeguard and my daughter Connie loves swimming. She used to come a lot when she was about 10. She used to like Callum the lifeguard and enjoyed pushing him in – he was a great lifeguard.

I love the lifeguards. They are my colleagues now, because I work in the cafe and it's been great getting to know them. When I first worked here four or five years ago, I loved it because I was in my 40s and suddenly had colleagues in their teens and 20s. That gives you a different perspective on the pool. They make the pool safe and they are part of the scene. They are usually young men and women and they are transitory, they are either at school or uni but they come back, you see them over the years. It's a big family.

Working in the cafe in the summer isn't as enjoyable as the winter because it's very busy, I work much longer hours and it's tiring. But it's lovely to see everyone queuing up for ice creams, and I try to get a swim at the end of a shift. I love the cafe because I get to know all the customers, especially in the winter. Most people are happy to chat and I harangue them with my views; I don't think I have offended many people. In the autumn, when the pool is closed in the middle of the day, I will swim on my own through the leaves, with the lifeguards keeping an eye on me. It's just very tranquil and lovely. It's my life.

ALEX BUXTON

In 1990, as lidos were lost across the UK, Jesus Green Lido seemed to be living on borrowed time. Lifelong water lover Alex Buxton explains why she set up the Friends of Jesus Green Open Air Pool and how she hopes the rise in cold water swimming will help sustain it.

STANDING IMPATIENTLY ON the lawn, I watched my father take an armful of floppy plastic and, puffing steadily, transform it into a bouncy circle. A hose was draped over the edge. Runnels of water nosed their way across the surface.

Slowly the bright blue paddling pool filled to the brim, the water crystal clear. In I plunged, a hot and tubby two-and-a-half year old. Thus began a lifelong love of all watery places.

Thirty years later, I bought a house in George Street, Cambridge, not knowing that just down the road, behind a hedge of leylandii, was one of the country's two longest pools. On a sweltering day, I walked through that now familiar gate to marvel at my luck. No showers, no cafe – but a perfect rectangle of glittery blue.

Perfect, but under threat. The 1980s were a desultory time for outdoor pools. Up and down the country lidos were shutting, filled in to make car parks or space for supermarkets, roofed over or simply abandoned. In the hot summer of 1990, it seemed that Jesus Green Outdoor Pool too was on borrowed time.

Cambridge City Council, forced to make cutbacks, proposed shortening the season to save money. This measure, we swimmers feared, would be the first slippery step to closing the pool for good. Someone needed to do something.

I'd never organised a group of any kind. I hadn't a clue how to launch a campaign and hated the thought of public speaking. But three of us (Elaine White, Bronwen Dinneen and I) collaborated over a series of meetings in each other's houses to set up a group to make our voices heard.

We named ourselves Friends of Jesus Green Open Air Pool. It sounds

> **" In I plunged, a hot and tubby two-and-a-half year old. Thus began a lifelong love of all watery places**

impressive but it was simply a list of names and addresses. No fee to join, though some lovely people gave us money for stamps. We chose Friends because that's what we were – and friends are what we need.

Together we wrote letters, we spoke to councillors. We organised parties, competitions and outings. We produced T-shirts. Local press helped and the season (May to September) remained unaltered. But a series of dismal summers saw the future of the pool continue to hang in the balance.

It takes a stretch of imagination to remember just how few people swam in cold, or even cool, water. One grey

evening 25 years ago, I went for a swim in the early evening and was told by the lifeguard Ed Durrant that I was only the second person to swim that day.

Then, a miracle. Cold water swimming became a thing. In August 2021, Cambridge City Council voted unanimously for the pool to remain open for the very first time through the bitter months. Frost sparkled on the steps. Lifeguards cradled mugs of tea. New friendships were forged on the benches, in the showers, in the sauna.

How grateful we are for all the support we have from far and wide. From Cambridge City Council, from the pool operators, from everyone who comes to swim. How fabulously lucky we are to have this very special place.

It's funny to think that Jesus Green pool began life a century ago as the 'Corporation Bath'. It later became a 'Bathing Pool'. Today it's elevated to the giddy status of Lido. A tad too fancy perhaps, but it doesn't matter one iota. Jesus Green Lido, we love you.

NICKY BLANNING

Nicky Blanning has been coming to Jesus Green Lido since the 1960s. She swims every day and – whether it's 110 lengths or one – always feels better afterwards. She talks about the Lido's community, its voice and the legacy of the centenary, her hopes for the newly-established Friends of Jesus Green Lido charity and why, every day, she thanks her lucky stars for the Lido.

MY INVOLVEMENT WITH the Friends of Jesus Green Lido came not long after Alex Buxton set it up in the late 1980s because the Lido was on the brink of closure. When that threat passed, Alex stepped down as chair of the Friends and the group became less proactive.

Some years ago some of us felt we should ensure the Friends' longevity, so that should a new crisis emerge we'd be better prepared and so we could think about raising funds for the pool, but mainly as a way to build relationships with Cambridge City Council (which owns Jesus Green Lido) and Better (the current operator). It's essential they hear a voice from users.

The use of Jesus Green Lido has changed since Covid. Outdoor swimming and cold water swimming have become much more popular as we've realised their impact on mental health. It's late October and there are far more young people, students in particular, swimming here now; that would never have happened in the past.

The Friends has evolved too. We've become more organised, we have an active committee, we've got a fabulous new website, and the three words we decided summed up our purpose – community, voice and legacy – are really important.

Anybody can join the Friends and it's free to join. You simply sign up on the website and receive newsletters, updates and details of upcoming events.

The Lido is a community. I always refer to 'users' rather than 'swimmers' because not everyone who comes here swims, and we have to remember that. For me, the community here is like a second family. Coming here feels like coming to another home: it's so important to me, I could not live without it and I know that lots of other people feel the same.

We have regular lunch and afternoon events where everybody brings and shares food. They're really popular and a great way of bringing people together. It's a chance to see swimmers you might miss because they swim at different times, an opportunity to get together and enjoy the space.

We have a 'Lido Tourists' WhatsApp group to encourage people to visit other lidos and report on them. One of the things we'd like to do is develop a twinning programme with groups at other lidos in the UK, Europe and beyond. There's an annual trip to Felixstowe (previously we went to Dunwich) in October, at the end of the summer season. That has been taking place for many years.

Voice is about speaking up on behalf of Lido users. Making sure the Lido remains in the public eye and that users have a good relationship with the Council and the operator. And legacy is ensuring this

> **Winter swimming here has become popular and it's important because not everyone feels safe swimming the in river**

Friends of Jesus Green Lido bring and share New

place thrives for the next 100 years or more.

The Friends plays a very important role in speaking up for people. We don't assume that everyone thinks the same way, so we're here to listen to people's ideas and take them forward, and ensure that everybody has an opportunity to say their piece.

Part of our legacy is that in 2023 – the Lido's centenary year – we set up a Friends of Jesus Green Lido charity. A few of the Friends volunteered to be trustees and our aims will be fundraising and trying to realise the ambitions of the Friends of Jesus Green Lido committee. For example, if the Friends said they'd like a new cafe opening onto both the pool and Jesus Green, that would be our focus. We'll be running a survey to find out what Lido users would like to see in the future.

The centenary celebrations brought together different people with different skills with great enthusiasm. From the centenary day itself at the end of August, to two performances of the play *Nothing great is easy*, an open-air film night, a new short film on the Lido by Tanya Jones, a new gardening group, new signage, an installation by Cambridge Yarn Collective, a tile project, and the wonderful flags designed by first-year illustration students at Anglia Ruskin University. The flags are extraordinary and they make me happy every time I see them.

We had a specially composed piece of music by Tom Ling performed by the Chesterton Community College wind band on Midsummer's Eve, and of course the Centenary Cygnets synchronised swimmers, of which I'm a part.

Both my parents were very good swimmers and we swam outdoors from a very young age. They had access to

Year party, January 2023

an outdoor pool in woodland belonging to people they knew in Oxfordshire. We went there regularly; it's where I learned to swim as I didn't have formal lessons. When I was young, I swam competitively at school and county level – but backstroke, which I rarely swim now. I've swum almost every day, all my life.

I've been coming here since the late 1960s. My godmother, my mother's best friend, lived in Cambridge. We'd visit often and the instinct was to come to water so we'd swim at Jesus Green Lido or the Abbey, which was then an outdoor pool.

My first impression of Jesus Green was overwhelming and is still very clear. It was just huge – beyond huge, beyond imagination – for a small child seeing this enormous pool with its diving boards. Even though I was a competent swimmer, getting into such a large pool and swimming this huge distance was daunting. But it was wonderful too. Although the atmosphere was different, it still had this body of very enthusiastic people, lots of families, with lots of noise and laughter. I remember the sweet shop which was off-limits to us, my mother was very strict about it.

I moved to Cambridge in the mid-1980s and married my husband who's an academic. I swam at Jesus Green every day during the season and then indoors in winter, which I never enjoyed as much. But I loved coming to Jesus Green, and I have many long-standing friendships from swimming both here and in the river.

Swimming in the River Cam is a different experience. I do put my face in the water, but I tend to swim breaststroke more and am more observant of my surroundings, the trees and the wildlife. I always look out for a kingfisher and seeing one brings me complete joy. I love being able to swim in the Lido and in the river, and we're really fortunate to have access to both. Even more so now the Lido is open in winter. For me, that's a godsend; I think it is for everybody. Winter swimming here has become popular and it's important because not everyone feels safe swimming the river. That's why I'd like to see the Lido open every day throughout the year.

I swim many more lengths in summer, and as the temperature drops the distance declines. The maximum I've done in a day is 110 lengths (10km) but usually I swim between 22 and 30 lengths in summer and between 6 and 14 lengths in winter. If I swim less than 6 I feel I haven't really swum, unless it's frozen and we're only allowed to swim in a fraction of the pool.

There's something glorious about swimming outside which you don't get in an indoor pool. The fact the pool is so long means you can really get into your stroke and it brings out my competitive nature because I'm usually aiming at someone to reach and overtake. It's a little target, a little goal.

I love the movement through water, its silkiness. It's real magic and there is nothing like it. When I come out – even

Nicky Blanning, right, with Annie Morgan James

if I've only had time for a length – I've never regretted it. It's always worth the effort of changing. And I always feel better afterwards – even if I'm frozen. I always changed in the cubicles, but in the past two years I've switched to poolside changing. You can chat to people, get offered a cup of tea – it's more social, less insular.

I tend to dive or jump in rather than using the steps and then swim hell-for-leather. I swim in the middle lane because I never learned to breathe on both sides. I breathe to my right so in the fast lane I've occasionally hit the steps with my hand.

I've got two children and swam throughout my later pregnancy. Tom, my eldest, is 22. He was born in June – I had contractions in the Lido, which concerned the lifeguards. I remember them asking if I should really be swimming. I remember smiling and saying I was fine, but actually feeling that I needed to push… but Mary Williams was on hand, and I made it to the hospital in time.

Tom first swam in the Lido when he

was two months old – I wanted him to experience water very young. There were some lovely ladies here who'd push or carry him round the pool, talking to him and showing him the trees and sky while I swam. They were incredibly generous with their time, they let me swim in peace, which was wonderful, although breastfeeding wasn't easy then – I had to hide in a cubicle – hopefully that's more relaxed now.

I remember lots of swimmers, people like Arthur Mansfield. He'd often give me advice on my stroke and ask others to watch me. He was such a nice man, so keen on swimming and for people to learn to swim and swim well. I can still picture him on the side of the pool.

Leila Brown (an academic) was another regular. Like Arthur, she came to Jesus Green Lido from the 1920s until her death in early 2010s. She still came regularly, even after a serious injury meant she needed help to get in – a remarkable woman.

A friend I met through swimming, Kevan Hayward, died suddenly six years ago just after turning 50. His widow Michelle generously gave funds raised at his funeral to the Friends of Jesus Green Lido. That enabled us to commission a memorial board from Rowan (an arts centre and forest school for adults with learning disabilities) to remember people who had long connections with the pool.

I think we should appreciate the Lido every day and appreciate having it through the seasons, through summer into autumn, winter and back to spring. We should look at the sky, the lime trees and the changing seasons. Every day, I thank my lucky stars for the Lido.

VAL MOORE

Val Moore is a swimmer, a lifeguard and a coach. Jesus Green Lido means different things in each of her roles.

OPEN WATER SWIMMING here. Not quite 'free range,' or 'off piste', but as close as it gets. Feel the chop, the blue depth, the extra focus to finish the length. Tuck in behind or overtake. Chat, recover, or plough through a cold, counted 5km. Only your thoughts, but never alone.

Watching. Who has just entered? What might happen here? How long in the water? Endlessly inspirational swimmers, families and colleagues. Taking action, often when people least expect. Being their safety net.

Your ambition? How does your swimming feel, look and compare? Swim with you. Capture your improvements. Make a plan together, and to find others to share the journey. Review, and go again. Achieving what felt impossible. We love open water swimming.

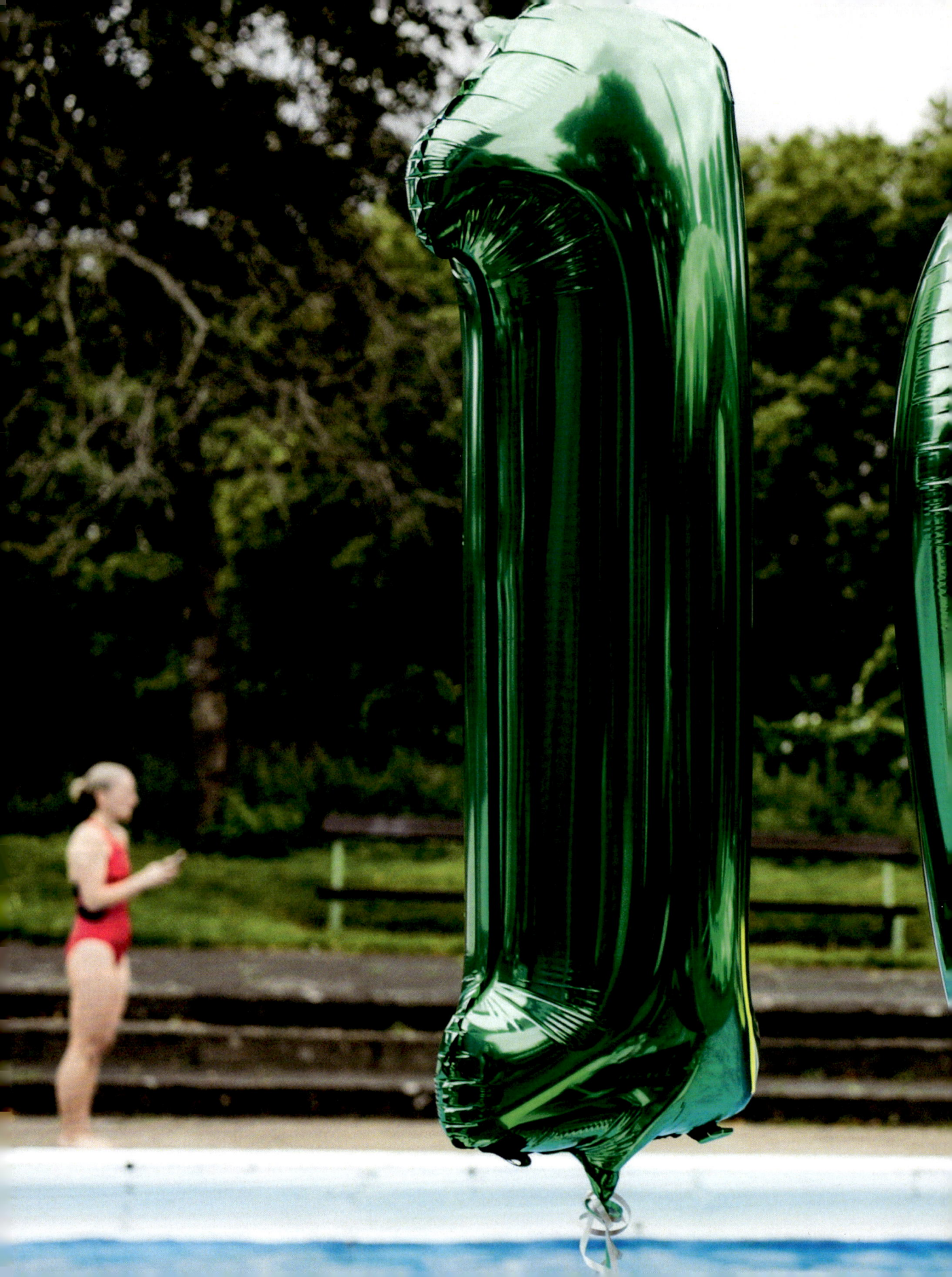

CELEBRATIONS

A year of events was held to celebrate the centenary of Jesus Green Lido, from the arrival of knitted penguins to cinema and musical performances. There was even some synchronised swimming!

APRIL: THE LIDO IN BLOOM

WE STARTED OUR centenary year by getting Jesus Green Lido ready for a summer of celebrations. Wanting to make the most of our natural surroundings, lifeguard Kane Smith set up a new gardening group. In April and May, green-fingered swimmers set about weeding, planning and planting new flower beds, pots and hanging baskets. In the autumn, they planted bucketloads of bulbs to herald the spring.

"I'm loving being part of the gardening group at the Lido; there's a great sense of camaraderie and it feels good to be doing something tangible towards the centenary celebrations and beyond," said Sylvia Dannreuther, who has swum at Jesus Green for 15 years and celebrated her 50th birthday at the Lido.

"The gardening project has come at just the right time for me; I've been a professional gardener and planting designer for 15 years, and although I retired recently, I'm still very keen to be involved with all things horticultural, increasingly from the angle of encouraging biodiversity."

MAY: CENTENARY SIGNAGE

TO WELCOME SWIMMERS through the turnstiles – and provide a backdrop for celebratory selfies – we asked Cambridgeshire signwriter Carlie Allan of Buck & Bear to design and paint a new sign celebrating the Lido's centenary.

Film night at Jesus Green Lido

"There's clearly a community of people who swim here often and know each other. Swimmers came to talk to me and take photos – it's lovely to have your work appreciated," said Carlie.

"I really wanted to take on this project as it was such a community-driven idea. I've always lived in Cambridgeshire, so I love the idea of being part of something 'Cambridge' and celebrating the Lido's history and centenary.

"Being part of something iconic, historic and much loved is the best feeling."

JUNE: POOLSIDE PENGUINS

ON A HOT, sunny day in June, the Cambridge Yarn Collective installed a trio of crochet penguins (which first appeared on Jesus Green's tennis courts to raise awareness of their status as an endangered species) near the pump room.

Sophie Neville, Dorothy Singer, Clare Collier and Hilary Butler set up the Cambridge Yarn Collective six years ago after working on a project for Cambridge Junction.

"We love making big, free, public artworks for all to enjoy. We love making colourful, joyful artworks that make people smile. And we love working with friends, collaborating and being creative," said Dorothy.

Installing the penguins was the first time the Collective visited the Lido, Dorothy added. "Seeing it so busy and enjoyed by so many on a hot day really tempted us to dip a toe in the water."

JUNE: *NOTHING GREAT IS EASY* MAKES A BIG SPLASH

JUNE AND AUGUST saw actor Chris Hudson take the plunge with his watery, wonderful one-man show, *Nothing great is easy*, at the Lido.

The two sell-out performances told the remarkable story of the intrepid Captain Webb, the first person to swim the English Channel. In this heroic story of ups and downs, Chris brought Captain Webb to life, diving into the water and delivering his lines in and out of the pool.

The show got a rave review in the *Cambridge News*: "Director Rosina Piovani's simple but effective staging made excellent use of the Lido setting, with Webb frequently diving into the pool to demonstrate his technique, holding his breath beneath the water then re-emerging to seamlessly continue his narration."

A huge thankyou to everyone who came along to the play, to Chris Hudson of Historyonics Theatre Company, director Rosina Piovani and producer Antony Quinn for a memorable performance.

JUNE: MOONLIT SWIMS

JESUS GREEN LIDO marked midsummer with two iconic swims. On 21 June, the summer solstice, the Lido was open from sunrise to sunset with live music by the Chesterton Community College fiddle band. Led by Penny Veryard, the performance included the world premiere of Tom Ling's *In at the deep middle*, a piece specially commissioned for the Lido's centenary.

Olympic medalist Cassie Patten ran a freestyle masterclass at the Lido in July

Then, on 24 and 25 June 2023, competitive swimmers had a unique opportunity to experience an overnight swim at Jesus Green Lido. The dusk-to-dawn swim began as the sun set at 9pm, with relay teams swimming through the night before celebrating the sunrise at 4.30am.

AUGUST: ENCHANTED CINEMA BRINGS *JAWS* TO THE LIDO

AUGUST SAW ANOTHER sellout event – this time an Enchanted Cinema screening of the oceanic epic *Jaws* plus the premiere of *A year in the life of the lido*, a film by Tanya Jones and students at Hills Road Sixth Form College.

AUGUST: FLYING THE FLAG FOR JESUS GREEN LIDO

IN AUGUST, 30 fabulous flags designed by local art students were installed in and around Jesus Green Lido. A key part of the centenary celebrations, the flags were commissioned by Better, Cambridge City Council and Friends of Jesus Green Lido from first-year BA Illustration students at Anglia Ruskin University. We asked them for eye-catching designs that celebrated the centenary and reflected the Lido's values – community, voice and legacy.

"We had a series of meetings with the students, telling them about the Lido's history and sharing old photos of the pool. They then visited the Lido to experience its amazing atmosphere and wonderful community for themselves," Caroline Lewis from the Friends of Jesus Green Lido explained.

"The project has been great for both students and swimmers. The students gained valuable experience working to a brief for real clients, and the flags are a brilliant addition to Jesus Green and the Lido."

AUGUST: HAPPY 100TH BIRTHDAY, JESUS GREEN LIDO!

THE SUN SHONE and crowds flocked to Jesus Green Lido to celebrate its 100th birthday on Bank Holiday Monday 28 August 2023.

Against strong competition, Catherine Hayhurst won the centenary cake competition, which was judged by Deputy Mayor of Cambridge Baiju Thittala Varkey, GB Paralympic athlete

Louis Rolfe and Channel swimmer Evie Anema.

Jesus Green Lido's very own synchro swimmers, the Centenary Cygnets, brought a touch of 1920s glamour to the pool for their first ever public performance. The nine-strong group hatched the plan in the winter over a post-swim cuppa, and the Cygnets' coach Beccy used YouTube to learn the moves. "The best thing about it is learning how to do backwards somersaults – and the giggling," said Cygnet Danya Harris.

OCTOBER: JESUS GREEN FRIENDS' FELIXSTOWE SEA SWIM

SOME 40 SWIMMERS swapped Jesus Green for Felixstowe in October for the Friends of Jesus Green Lido's annual sea swim. Welcomed with homemade flapjacks by Mayor of Felixstowe Seamus Bennett, their swim was bookended by morning coffee at Fludyers Hotel, fish and chips and afternoon tea!

JESUS GREEN LIDO: CAMBRIDGE 'PEOPLE'S POOL' TURNS 100
BY ORLA MOORE, BBC NEWS, CAMBRIDGE

JESUS GREEN LIDO in Cambridge is celebrating turning 100 years old – a year for every yard of its length. The Lido has a dedicated band of lifelong swimmers who have taken to the cold water here for decades. So what is its enduring appeal?

"You come through that turnstile and it's like a portal to a special place," Dr Annie Morgan James explains.

"Your problems are left outside and people welcome you – the pool welcomes you."

Jesus Green Lido lies parallel to the river Cam by Jesus Green Lock and offers a quiet idyll in the middle of the city.

It began life on 30 August 1923 as the Jesus Green Bath, a 100-yard (91m) long pool with two shallow ends and a deep centre.

The pool is the joint longest in the UK with Tooting Bec Lido in London.

Dr Morgan James is working on a history of the lido for its centenary year, drawing on the experiences of the people who use it. The pool was carved out, she says, by labourers who had returned from World War One.

"For the first 10 to 15 years it was filled with water from the river, in fact, people used to complain about the fish," she adds.

"But outdoor swimming in Cambridge goes right back to that period of time when the rules were written.

"In the 16th Century, a young scholar at St John's College called Everard Digby wrote of *The art of swimming* [the 1587 book, *De arte natandi*] which provided readers with the means to swim, illustrating strokes to stop people drowning.

"It was important because a lot of undergraduates were up to high jinks, jumping in the water."

Ruth Barnett, 75, of Cottenham, remembers learning to swim at Jesus Green Lido from the age of five.

"We went to school on Milton Road and mum would come and meet us in the summer with our lunch, bring us here – we would swim – go back to school and then after school we did the same again," she says.

She remembers how the Lido custodian both took the entry money and worked as the lifeguard, using a stick with a ring on in it to teach people how to swim.

Ms Barnett still comes to the lido every day and normally manages 18 lengths – when the water is warm enough.

"When you come through the gates you are in a different world," she says.

"It's Narnia. It's wonderful."

"It's my life, I love it – I've got to do it every day," says Victoria Bursa, 74.

"I have this big painting of a swimmer and when I wake up it's the first thing I see.

"It's the feeling of freedom in the water. I would recommend it, but not to too many people – I want it to myself," she adds.

Fellow regular Gregor Alvey recently turned 70 and marked the birthday milestone with a swim.

"I've been coming here since 1973 – it's a bit of a haven," he says. "I'm a retired teacher and I'd come down after work for the last half hour of the day.

"Down here, the bells don't ring and there was no one to tap you on the

Ruth Barnett learned to swim at Jesus Green Lido

shoulder and ask you for something. It was half an hour of mental freedom."

It is not just the visitors who love the Lido.

Lifeguard Finn Barnes, 24, from Cambridge, began occasional work at the Lido while studying at Swansea University.

He now manages the 20-strong poolside team which has four lifeguards on duty at any one time.

"I love the atmosphere – it's very chilled out – you're outside all the time," he says.

The Lido also hosts its own troupe of synchronised swimmers – the Centenary Cygnets.

Founder Danya Harris, 36, says she named the team after the baby swans on the Cam.

"After Covid there was a need for being outside and being around other people," she says. "I came here every day and became hooked on the whole cold water thing. There was a camaraderie."

Alexandra Buxton, 70, helped establish the first informal Friends of Jesus Green Lido in the 1980s. It was a time, she says, when support for cold water swimming was dwindling and lidos were closing. "I'm addicted to swimming in cold water – I've always liked swimming in rivers and the sea," she says.

"There was a book called *Waterlog* by Roger Deakin that made people realise they weren't alone in their love for swimming in rivers – it sparked a revolution and resurgence in cold water swimming.

"Here, it's the length of the pool, the surroundings, the lovely community of people – it's a place where people make friends."

Nicky Blanning, who chairs the 300-member Friends group, says: "It has a community spirit with a wonderful atmosphere.

"Our aim is to speak up for other users and be the liaison between Better [which operates the lido] and the city council who own it – and to ensure its longevity," she says.

Ms Blanning says there's "something so wonderful and invigorating" about swimming outside.

Those who hold the Lido close to their hearts are now looking forward to its next 100 years.

"This pool was built a decade before lidos became popular and it makes Jesus Green Bath ahead of its time," Dr Morgan James says.

"The 1920s was a time of great change, so the idea of this pool in a place like Cambridge that had a divided community of town and gown was key.

"It has remained a very special place in Cambridge.

"It's the people's pool."

From BBC News at www.bbc.co.uk/news/uk-england-cambridgeshire-66170456

CENTENARY CYGNETS

AN AD-HOC GROUP of synchronised swimmers formed over shivers and coffee during winter 2022: Beccy Taylor, Catherine Hayhurst, Danya Harris, Emily Manning, Esther Chambers, Nicky Blanning, Patsy Rathbone, Rosalie Woods (occasional coach), Sara Ledwith and Zoe Rose. On performance days they were brilliantly accompanied by sharks: Chris Hayhurst and Mez van Slageren.

We had the idea for synchronised swimming in the winter over a post-swim cup of tea. Some of the appeal was in the glitter and some in the pure silliness of the idea.

There are around nine of us and we're called the Centenary Cygnets, because we're not quite as elegant as swans yet, and one of our members was especially enchanted by the little fluffy cygnets on the River Cam this spring.

We performed the Dance of the Little Swans from *Swan Lake* and made our debut at Jesus Green Lido's centenary celebrations in August 2023 and – thanks to popular demand – made a second splash in mid-September.

We train at the Lido. Choreographer Beccy has learned the various moves from YouTube and then been our coach. We also got ideas and inspiration from other cold water synchro teams.

The best thing about it has been learning how to do backwards somersaults – and the giggling.

Chris Hudson performs his sell-out show

CHRIS HUDSON and ROSINA PIOVANI
NOTHING GREAT IS EASY

IN JUNE 2023, Jesus Green Lido kicked off its centenary celebrations with a sell-out performance of *Nothing great is easy* by the Cambridge-based Historyonics Theatre Company. Written and performed by Chris Hudson, and directed by Rosina Piovani, the play immersed the poolside audience in the extraordinary life of Captain Matthew Webb, who in 1875 became the first person to swim the English Channel.

ROSINA
If someone had told us that we would be performing the play in Cambridge's iconic Lido, two and a half years after starting rehearsals in January 2020, with a global pandemic in between, we would never have believed it.

After over a year of online and socially-distanced rehearsals, the show finally opened at Cambridge's Corpus Playroom in July 2021. Following the play's success at the Corpus, we performed it in several other venues in Cambridgeshire, and in early 2022 we heard that it might be possible to be part of Jesus Green Lido's centenary celebrations. We were truly honoured by the invitation.

For the first time, we had the chance to perform in Captain Webb's element – water It was a huge challenge to adapt the play for scenes in the pool but somehow it felt natural, almost like it should have always been like that.

As a director, it was an exciting proposition and I immediately took the plunge to put on a play using a 100-yard-long pool as a stage. There were so many new challenges – from positioning a poolside audience and capturing audio from mid-pool, to representing storms in the English Channel and directing an actor who is treading water.

Chris is an avid swimmer, which helped him endure scenes in the pool, keeping himself afloat while brilliantly becoming Captain Matthew Webb. Being able to rehearse at the pool was key, and we're grateful the lifeguards were willing to stay after closing time so we could have the pool to ourselves.

Both sold-out performances at the Lido surpassed our expectations. The audience immediately connected with the story; they cheered and clapped and became part of it, something we had not experienced when the play was done on dry land. It was beautiful to see the audience settling for a warm sunny evening, enjoying the golden hour as the play started and then becoming immersed in the action – the theatre communion between audience and actors in pure expression.

CHRIS

Six years ago, I'd never heard of Captain Webb. After reading several books on outdoor swimming, someone recommended that I read one on Webb. It was a true case of serendipity. I had been searching for a subject for a possible one-man show, and as soon as I finished reading about Webb's life, I knew I had found my guy.

There were so many aspects of Webb's life that I found fascinating: the incredible achievement of his Channel swim, the colourful characters who populated the Victorian swimming scene, his bizarre attempts to capitalise on his fame, and the ultimate tragedy of his final stunt. His story was compelling, but how could I make it work on stage?

The answer was in trusting my longtime collaborator Rosina Piovani. Faced with a 10,000-word script with no stage directions, Rosina somehow found a way for me to represent various swimming scenes on stage. We used physical theatre techniques and mime to allow me to help the audience suspend their disbelief and imagine they were seeing the good Captain swimming before their eyes.

By our first performance at the Corpus Playroom in Cambridge, I felt I'd got under Webb's skin, or perhaps vice versa. I have nowhere near his stamina or bravery, but his love of open water swimming, his wish to inspire youngsters to learn to swim and his desire to do something great were all aspects of his character that I could relate to. Attempting a one-man show felt like the acting equivalent of swimming the Channel!

After taking the show to different venues in 2021–22, we were delighted to get the chance to perform at Jesus Green, where I've had many happy swims in the past. It quickly became clear that Rosina wanted me to go into the water during the performance, despite the potential for jeopardy being higher than usual. I was unsure how my body and voice would react to the demands of projecting while swimming, and didn't know if I would stay warm enough to make it to the final scene. Some rehearsals ended with yellow fingers and water up my nose, as I discovered that trying to do an underwater somersault was not something

I should repeat before an audience *(unlike the Centenary Cygnets - ed)*.

On 10 June, the day of the first performance, we were very lucky with the weather. The air temperature peaked at 29C, giving the water a little more warmth than the previous evening, when I had been a little shivery at the end of our dress rehearsal. The warmer conditions and the even warmer response from the capacity crowd combined to stop me feeling cold during and after the performance. I will never forget the feeling of reaching the end of the show and knowing that somehow we had pulled it off. To be invited back for a return performance a couple of months later, and to sell out again, was the icing on the cake.

As a swimmer, and now as a performer, I feel a special connection with Jesus Green Lido. I'm so grateful to have had the opportunity to tell Captain Webb's story in the perfect setting, and can only thank the Friends of Jesus Green Lido, and especially our production manager Antony Quinn, for allowing us two magical evenings which are the highlights of my theatrical career.

https://historyonics.weebly.com

THE FLAG PROJECT

The Friends of Jesus Green Lido, together with Better and Cambridge City Council, commissioned first year illustration students at Anglia Ruskin University to design flags to fly during the centenary celebrations. More than 30 flags were installed around the pool and Jesus Green. Feedback has been overwhelmingly positive. Swimmers and those involved reflect on the project.

Flag by Harriet Smeaton

HAR HARI KAUR

HAVING SOME ART around the pool changes the whole atmosphere – it adds a dimension we're not used to sitting and engaging with.

I'm very chatty, I'll talk to everyone, but the flags have sparked conversations here at the pool that I've not had before and with people I've never met. They bring people together

Flag by Ciara Calthrop

Flag by Michael Tyrrell

because they're new and different. Talking about the art has been positive and uplifting, and the conversations delightful.

The flags have made us aware of the pool's centenary and reinforced something very fundamental about this space. Through art, we've connected with what an amazing place this is and has been. I'm blown away by it.

I love them all but I'd say one of my favourites is the feather flag with a figure in an orange bikini. I'm very short-sighted so I like the fact that it's big and uncomplicated, there's a naivety about it.

Everything about the flags at the Lido is wonderful and makes it more celebratory.

ELEANOR THOMAS

Our first sight of the Lido was when

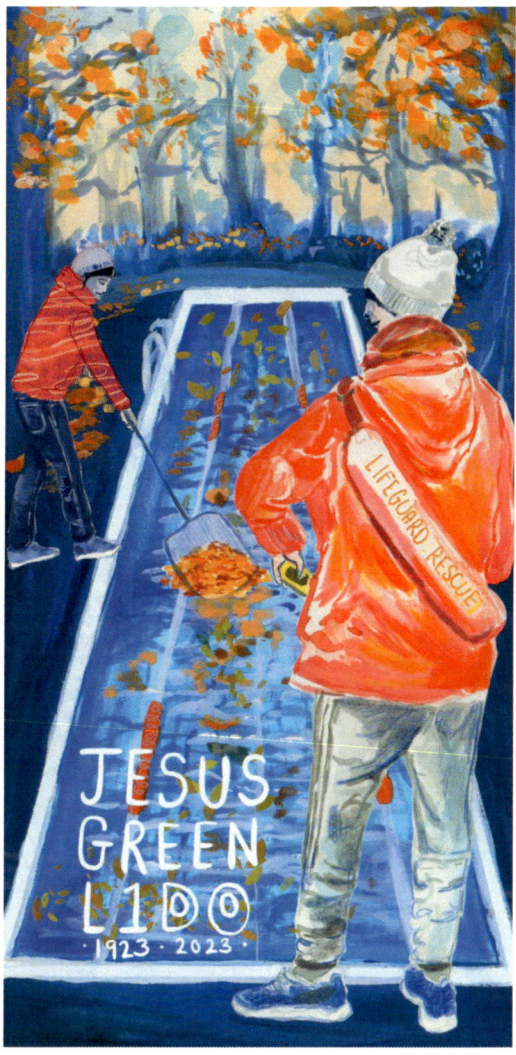

Flag by Eleanor Thomas

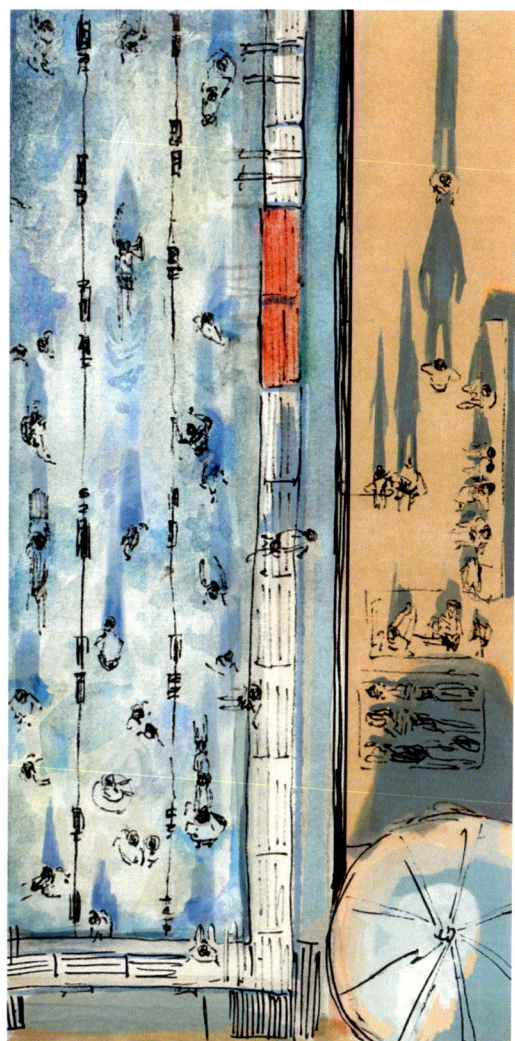

Flag by On Ki Angel Chak

Frances, our tutor, brought us down to the pool in March 2023. It was overcast and there were leaves in the pool. We met the Friends of Jesus Green Lido – who told us about the pool's history, its connection with Cambridge, and why it's still such an important place for people.

I think all of us picked up on the community, unity and legacy of the pool in our designs. That's why many of them show different perspectives and settings of the pool and its history.

In my design, I wanted to capture the fact that people swim here all year, in all weathers; it's not just a place for summer. I wanted to capture how beautiful it is, even in winter, when it's still full of life and community.

Working on the project has been an

Flag by Rebeca Olender

Flag by Percy Mourao

incredible experience. It's been really nice to connect with part of Cambridge, and our artwork reflects that. It was hard work but seeing our work shown around the pool and on Jesus Green means a lot, because I know how passionate everyone was about the project. When the Friends,

Better and Cambridge City Council came to ARU to see our designs they were in awe of what we'd done.

It feels amazing that our art can reflect the importance of the Lido for so many people, and that everyone can connect with it through our work. By

Flag by Poppy-Jo Bromige

Flag by Amealia Wharmby

illustrating different faces of the pool, our insights can show why this place is so important and why it's lasted for 100 years.

Before this project I didn't even know the Lido was here. That's why it's important that the flags are positioned along the paths across Jesus Green leading to the pool. I hope they spark curiosity and draw people here, people like me who didn't know. I hope the flags help people forge these new connections.

As I came here today, my fiancé and I

were walking down the path and saw the flags. Seeing mine was really exciting. Even if people don't know that the pool is here, they'll see the flags and wonder what's going on, and hopefully that will bring them back to the pool. I know I'll come back, because this place is important to me now. I've given my art and my perspective of the pool to the community and I've gained something in return. We're all proud to have helped communicate people's love of the pool.

As a practising illustrator it's given me experience of working with a client on a brief. And I've gained insight into how illustration can benefit people and help draw people together. The brief about the project said the work should reflect the year-round nature of the pool. That's why I chose to focus one of my designs on winter and another in autumn with a lifeguard picking up the leaves.

Monoprinting features across all three of my designs. It gives the pool an icy feel but one that still flows. And I wanted there to be pops of colour as contrast, and to pick out the shower block with the stripes. The red lines on the edge of the pool connect with the river boats. You can tell it's winter but the complementary colours show that it's still Jesus Green Lido.

My designs are a mixture of prints, painting techniques and digital. That's how I like to work, painting something and then digitally editing and enhancing it. A lot of us like mixing traditional techniques into our work – they bring originality and a sense of organicness.

For the base painting, I used gouache and then digitally edited it with Procreate, which is where I introduced the monoprint and text and added the textures of the trees. And there's a little snowman, which I saw on the Lido's Instagram. I wanted to include it because even in winter people are here swimming, people are having fun, it's a place people can come all year round.

The project has connected me to this place, not just through my art but through conversations with people here about the passion people have for this environment.

MICHAEL TYRRELL

THE DESIGN FOR my flag is a top-down view of the pool flowing into the river. I like to combine digital and traditional techniques in my work. This design is based on scanned photos, and coloured using an old photo of the Lido, so it has history baked into it.

It was an exciting project and unlike anything I'd done before. It was stressful but really rewarding, a great opportunity and I'm proud of our work.

I am far from athletic. Although we came for a site visit in cold weather, I might be persuaded to come back and have a dip!

ZOE MOGRIDGE

THE PROJECT WORKED brilliantly because the students have a slightly different lens through which they view the Lido. For them, it's all about storytelling.

FRANCES IVES

I'M SO PROUD of our students' work on Jesus Green Lido's centenary flag project.

TANYA JONES

THE IDEA FOR the centenary film was born out of a serendipitous chat with Annie Morgan James in September 2022. We talked about our love of lidos – Jesus Green in particular – and the centenary that would be happening in 2023. By the end of the conversation, I'd offered to make a film.

My love affair with Jesus Green Lido began a long time ago. I must have first walked through the turnstiles in the late 1980s, beguiled I'm sure by the sight of blue water and diving boards. The turnstile is still a gateway to something special – another world where time often seems to stop or not really exist at all.

The Lido feels out of time. It is a tranquil blue lagoon amid a busy city. What often strikes me most when I'm there is its sound palette. Birds and water take the place of the traffic and hubbub of the city centre. I love the rich, vibrant noises of Cambridge but also need the metronomic gentle splashing of the swimmers, the calling of birds to one another and the soft exchanges of chat and laughter provided at the Lido to give balance.

In the film, I wanted to tell the story of what the Lido means to its community, and to give a sense of what a beautiful and inclusive place it is. I gave myself the task of creating a film which took the viewer through the seasons and would be structured around a series of interviews where I asked people to tell me what the Lido meant to them.

The Lido is very beautiful. Blue dominates, with reds, browns and greens following. The scale of the pool gives it azure dominance in the frame, and the green and white shower blocks, brown wooden changing hut walls and red poolside diving stripe beautifully animate its edges.

It is an easy place to film because it has all angles and distances covered. Long shots down the length of the pool, close-ups of leaves on water or mid shots of the cafe are all packed with depth and colour and accompanied by a wonderful ambient soundtrack. The camera doesn't have to create this world and neither does the editing software – this is the real and magical space that is Jesus Green Lido.

So, who are the characters that populate this stage? Who are the people who love this world? They are everybody and all of us. It was a joy and a privilege to speak to the people who participated in the centenary film. They were generous and candid with their stories of what the Lido meant to them. Some were regular swimmers and for one it was her first trip, accompanied by her mum.

Each story is the same but different. The joy that the Lido brings, the solace, the feeling of belonging and the way in which a swim can transform a mundane day into a wonderful one – these are the themes that thread through the different interviews. I listened and filmed as individuals shared how one place can mean so much to so many.

The cutaway footage of lifeguards going about their tasks, drinks and snacks being sold, swimmers in wetsuits or bobble hats and people relaxing by the pool in the sunshine all wordlessly match the messages from the interviews; this is a community space for everyone, throughout the year.

Sitting in an edit suite at Hills Road Sixth Form College with some of my Film and Media A level students, I put the story together. Colleagues came in to look and all said the same thing, "How joyful! It makes me want to go there." It is a joyful film because the people and the place in it are marked by joy. We've been lucky enough to have Jesus Green Lido for 100 years. Let's hope that this very special place will be here to offer peace and happiness for many years to come.

https://jesusgreenlido.org/film-celebrates-lidos-centenary-and-character/

LEIGH CHAMBERS

IT HAD BEEN some time since I'd been to the Lido before my visit in 2023. Both my daughters are grown up now, but I remember taking them to the Lido during the summer, having picnics on the grass and bringing them home, blue-lipped but tired and happy. Returning in April 2023 to interview users for a documentary I was making about the Lido for Cambridge 105 Radio, I realised I had forgotten just how much of an oasis in the city it is.

The air, the colours, all feel different once you're through those turnstiles. There's the constant gentle 'shush' of the water as swimmers plough up and down, the reflected light dappling on the stone, trees rustling, gentle conversation and the smell of a cheese and tomato toastie. An absolute festival for the senses.

And while I had expected the conversations I had for the documentary with pool users and those who work there to be about the benefits of cold water swimming, history and – yes – even community, what shone through was the love the swimmers have for the Lido. And so, unexpectedly and rather beautifully, it became a programme about love. Love for the place, the history, the community, with not a dissenting voice to be heard. A rare thing indeed.

TOM LING

Tom Ling is a Cambridge resident and a regular summer swimmer at the Lido. An accomplished fiddle player and composer, Tom can often be seen performing with Jon Betmead (folk singer/songwriter) in and around Cambridge. In honour of the Lido centenary, Tom composed In at the deep middle. *This beautiful piece celebrates the uniqueness of our pool with its deep middle and two shallow ends and is a perfect musical tribute, melodic and lyrically uplifting.*

IN AT THE DEEP MIDDLE BY TOM LING

© Tom Ling – April 2023

Acknowledgements

A HUGE THANK you to everyone who contributed to this book: to the swimmers who shared their stories; Sara Ledwith and Colin Campbell for editing and design; Anglia Ruskin University, Better, Cambridge City Council, and the Friends of Jesus Green Lido for funding; Jacqueline Mordue at the Cambridgeshire Collection; Francis Jeans, Martin Bond, Rebecca Chicot, Kane Smith, Danya Harris, Glenn Dakin and Andy Bonnett for artwork; Sarah Etchells and Matt Biss for meeting space and tech skills; and Piers Brendon for suggesting that our 100-year old, 100-yard pool, should be celebrated this way.

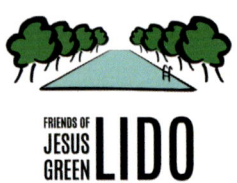

Images & Illustrations

We would like to thank the following photographers and artists for their kind permission to use their material on the following pages:

Martin Bond: Front and Back Cover, and pages 37, 60, 78-79, 81, 85, 92-93, 96, 107, 108, 111, 127, 131, 138, 161, 192
Andy Bonnett: 135, 159
Cambridge Collection: iv, xii-1, 3, 5, 6, 10-11, 12, 13, 24
Cambridge Evening News: 23, 137
Cambridge Swimming Company: 28-29, 99, 193
Rebecca Chicot: 26-27, 43, 47
Glenn Dakin: 35, 47, 76, 82, 113, 140
Danya Harris: 21, 34, 38, 52, 54, 56, 73, 90, 100, 150, 162, 165, 171, 173, 175, 178, 192-3
Francis Jeans: 103-105
Jane Keate: 95
Kane Smith: 30, 45, 48-49, 50, 51, 64-65, 82, 88-89, 98, 114-115, 141, 143, 145, 146, 148, 152, 154, 155, 158, 168-169, 170, 172, 173, 174, 192-3

Caption for pages 92-93: Emma Bateman, left, and Barbara Johnson

References

1 Ronald Westbrook, Jesus Green Pool in Lifeguard and other poems about a swimming pool (Westbrook Publications, Little Shelford, Cambridge, 2002).
2 Nicholas Orme, Early British Swimming 55BC – AD1719. With the First Swimming Treatise in English, 1595 (University of Exeter, 1983). p.86.
3 Howard Means, Splash: 10,000 Years of Swimming, (Allen & Unwin, London, 2020), pp.64-65
4 https://ww.christs.cam.ac.uk/facilities/swimming-pool (Accessed: 30 April 2024) https://www.emma.cam.ac.uk/members/blog/?id+463 (Accessed: 30 April 2024)
5 Roger Deakin. Waterlog: A Swimmer's Journey through Britain, (London: Vintage Books, 200) pp. 43-45.
6 Charles Sprawson, Haunts of the Black Masseur: The Swimmer as a Hero, (London: Jonathan Cape, 1992) p.19.
7 Christopher Love, A Social History of Swimming in England, 1800-1918: Splashing in the Serpentine, (London: Routledge, 2008) p.100.
8 Ibid; p.14.
9 Jean Perraton, Swimming Against the Stream: Reclaiming our Lakes and Rivers for People to Enjoy, (John Carpenter Publishing, 2005) pp. 20-21.
10 Jack Overhill, Cambridge at War: The Diary of Jack Overhill 1939-1945, Peter Searby (ed.) (Cambridge: Cambridge Records Society, 2010) p. 9.
11 Christopher Love. Op.Cit. pp. 14-15.
12 Agnes Campbell in Ibid; p.137.
13 The Minute Books (1920-1929) Cambridge Commons and Centenary Committee
14 The Cambridge Daily, January 3, 1923.
15 'Why not Mixed Bathing' in Cambridge Chronicle and University Journal, 3 January 1923.
16 Ibid.
17 Tim. Verney, 'Our intrepid reporter tries out the water' in Cambridge Evening News, 13 September 1981.
18 Alexandra Buxton, 'Birthday time at much loved oasis' in Cambridge Evening News, 31 July 1998.
19 Ibid.
20 Ibid.
21 Peter Pugh, Headline Britons 1921-1925, (London: Icon Books Ltd, 2017) p.14.
22 Janet Smith, Liquid Assets: The lidos and open-air swimming pools of Britain, (London: English Heritage, 2005) p.18.
23 Cambridge Daily News, Jesus Green Bath, 2 May 1924.
24 Ibid.
25 Roger Deakin. Op. Cit. p.41.
26 Jack Overhill, The Millstream, 1984, p.25. Cambridgeshire Collection, Cambridge Central Library.
27 Cambridge Town Owl. (2016) Cambridge at War – Jack Overhill's Diaries. Available at: https//lostcambridge.wordpress.com/2016/09/17/cambridge-at-war-jack-overhill's-diaries/ (Accessed: 31 October 2023).
28 THE FOUR-YEAR-OLDER - British Pathé (britishpathe.com) (Accessed: 9 May 2024)
29 Jack Overhill, The Millstream, 1984, p.57. Cambridgeshire Collection, Cambridge Central Library.
30 Ibid: p.57.
31 John Gaskell, Pool Complaints 'unfair to staff', Cambridge Evening News, 14 July 1976.
32 Sally Smith, Soldiers Step in to Man the City Pool, Cambridge Evening News, 17 June 1987.
33 BBC Cambridgeshire, interview with Chris Cox, Director, Jesus Green Pool https://www.bbc.co.uk/cambridgeshire/content/articles/2005/07/12/film_festival_jesus_green_feature.shtml (Accessed:14 November 2023).
34 Chris Havergal, Lido lands cameo role as floating film festival venue, Cambridge News, 7 September 2010.
35 Roger Deakin, Summertime Blues, The Telegraph, 17 June, 2020. https://www.telegraph.co.uk/travel/destinations/europe/uk/722522/UK-Summertime-blues.html [Accessed: 15 March 2023]
36 Christopher Beanland, Lido, (London: Batsford 2020) p.10.